ZANUSSI & JACK

EDNA CLYNE-REKHY

It has taken over ten years to write this book.

This is a selection of stories and events about dealing with a dementia patient.

Jack was an extremely intelligent man who eleven years ago started to show disturbing signs of Dementia.

Zanussi came into our lives unexpectedly in the most distressing circumstances.

His friendship and protection of Jack are a blessing.

TABLE OF CONTENT

MEGAN AND ZANUSSI

One

———— ◆ ————

J ack had been hankering for nearly twelve years to buy a house in Spain. I was reluctant to leave our beautiful house at the mouth of the River Brora in Sutherland. I loved how we could sit on the long window seat and watch the seals lying on the river bank at the bottom of our garden. Silently watch the ducks and wild fowl floating around and feeding as the tide ebbed and flowed.

We had managed to save so many Mallard ducklings from the marauding seagulls. Now we had a hungry flock of over a hundred. Jack fed them all every morning on a mixture of mashed, boiled potatoes and vegetables, left over toast, brown bread and oatmeal and porridge oats. After dropping their poo's all over the front lawn and the drive, they would follow him like the Pied Piper, along the road, down to the harbour and take flight into the river when he threw the food into the water.

One morning he took a little while longer to appear. I had left the door open when I came inside. They wandered in one by one, en mass, flying up onto the sofas in the lounge, padding across the dining table and peering out of the windows. Perching on the window seats, wandering through the hall, curiously pecking at the bottom of the curtains on the way to the conservatory. The whole journey splattered with slimy dark green and white poo's. I was making the beds upstairs when I heard all the quacking and rushed down to investigate. I unintentionally spooked the ducks and they flew in all directions, ornaments were knocked to the floor, poo splattered on the walls and windows. The hall was a long narrow corridor so it was impossible to escape the fluttering wings and hysteria. I managed to get into the conservatory and throw the door open wide. One by one they all fled through the gap to safety, after shooing them out of the lounge, kitchen and hall. My hair was straggling over my face, my clothes were spattered with duck poo and I ended up lying on the conservatory floor, having slid there on more of the slimy green and white droppings.

The excitement ended and I dragged myself on to a chair. Jack appeared from the bathroom, wide eyed in sheer amazement. "Has something exploded" he remarked, "I thought I heard a quacking sound". Needless to say, we were careful not to leave the door open again at duck feeding time.

I finally agreed to leave Brora after a particularly stormy night, when the high tide brought the sea right up to the conservatory door. We now felt unsafe to stay there and felt it was only a matter of time before we would be flooded, as a result of global warming. Now was the time to house hunt in Spain.

We managed to sell our house quickly and flew to Spain after contacting an estate agent there. We spent several exhausting days looking at prospective properties in some of the inland mountainous areas. Eventually we found a magnificent five bed roomed mountain villa, encased in three huge terraces, above the village of Muro de Alcoy in the Sierra Mariolas in Alicante state. This is in the National Park where all the wild life is protected. As we drove up the twisting mountain road, Jack and I looked at one another and said simultaneously "I feel we have been here before" When we drove into the large garden area, again we had the same feelings.

We were enthralled by the beauty of the villa and the views over the mountains, lakes and white villages. It was a spectacular vista.

The vendors welcomed us warmly and after viewing the house, huge garden, complete with granny cottage, large swimming pool and six olive and almond groves, we made the momentous decision that this would be our new home in Spain. We would now become olive farmers.

We sat down with the estate agent and the vendors to have coffee on the front terrace.

The strangest thing happened; I heard my Mother's voice say very clearly "Get up and look at the view" (my mother died five years before). I walked over to the garden fence, looked over the edge, down the mountain and suddenly felt my mother standing behind me. She slipped her arms around my waist, just like she had done so many times when I was a child. I could feel her give me a hug and the sensation passed. I was so overwhelmed, I burst into tears.

I turned round to see everyone watching me. Jack came over quickly and asked why I was crying. "Nana has just hugged me and I know it's going to be good for us here" "Okay" he said, "Let's buy it" and the decision was made to settle in Spain.

Two

---◆---

My elderly Mum lived with me for several years after she was unable to live in her own home. The whole family called her Nana, because all of her grandchildren called her that, we just followed suit. We often talked about the subject of crossing over and how it could be proven that there was a life hereafter. We were both sitting in the garden looking out on to the river and I said, "wouldn't it be wonderful if we could come back and let the family know that we were safe and happy." She replied, "Well! I'll come back as a butterfly on the day you bury me and if you go first, you come back as a butterfly" We both thought this was a great idea but it was a bit risky in case a passing bird ate us on the way. We laughed a lot about our escapades as butterflies and finally agreed that we would tell no-one about our agreement, it would be our big secret.

My Mum died on the eighteenth of December 2000. She had been a resident in the Meadows Nursing home in Dornoch. Jack and I were on holiday in Benelmadina in Spain when the phone call came informing us that she had a massive stroke and was paralyzed down her left side.

We left Spain at midnight the same day and eventually arrived back in Dornoch twelve hours later.

We went straight to the Meadows and raised the night staff. I explained that we had come straight there after hiring a car from Glasgow airport and driven up through nightmare conditions. We were shown straight to Nana's room. My Mum was lying in bed on her back with her arms at her sides.

The nurse had explained that she probably wouldn't know we were here and she wouldn't move because of the paralysis.

I walked over to the bed, touched her arm and said "Nana, we are here at last"

She opened her eyes immediately as I bent over her. Both arms came up and she placed her arms gently round my neck. "Oh Nennie, I knew you would come".

I couldn't believe she had spoken. She hadn't called me Nennie since I was a very young child. I hugged her and told her I loved her. Her arms fell back on the bed and she slipped back onto her pillow and closed her eyes.

Nana lived for another eight days. We were not allowed to give her anything to eat or drink because there was a strong possibility she would choke. I kept dabbing her lips with cotton wool dipped in water. I kept thinking, "If I give her something to eat, she may come back to us," but the staff were adamant that we should not give her food. This was their normal policy for stroke patients.

Jack took care of everything at home while I stayed at the Meadows with Nana day and night, only rushing home to have a shower, change my clothes, and give Jack and the dogs a cuddle, then return to the nursing home.

My sister Morag rushed over from New York to be with us and from then on we stayed with her 24 hours a day. Morag suggested we light some candles and sing old Girl Guide songs and Christmas carols. Not only did this cheer us up but we both felt sure she could hear us.

Nana was blind in one eye; she had an operation several years before to remove a small tumor behind the eyeball. Her eyelid was permanently drooped, when I lifted her eye lid to carefully wash her eye, I could see that it was just like a white marble streaked with red and yellow marks.

Nana passed away on the eighteenth of December 2000. I was holding her in my arms. She gave a huge sigh and when I looked at her face, she was looking straight at me, through me and on to someone or something I couldn't see. She was smiling and both of her eyes were wide open and perfect!! I said "Oh! My God Nana! You can see where you're going!" She closed her eyes and crossed over. I held her for such a long time; I felt that if I held her long enough, she would come back to me. Morag had gone home for a short break and arrived back, just as I was laying Nana down on the bed. She just couldn't believe what I had seen.

We had made arrangements for Nana to lay in rest at Dornoch Cathedral but the superstar Madonna was marrying Guy Ritchie on the twenty second and their four month old son Rocco had been christened there on the previous day, we thought it better (with the approval of the matron) that Nana should lie at rest at the Meadows.

Nana was buried on the day before Christmas Eve in the old Petty church yard near Castle Stuart overlooking the Moray Firth. All day I looked for a butterfly. In the barn church, during the service and in the churchyard at the burial service. I even kept a lookout driving home but no butterfly was to be seen. I didn't really think she would come because it was so cold. Snow on the ground and heavy frost.

When we reached home, Jack lit the big log fire in the lounge and I started making something to eat.

The pain of losing Nana and the events of the day finally hit me and I just burst into floods of tears, sobbing uncontrollably. Jack came over and wrapped his arms round me and held me until the grief subsided.

Suddenly, I felt Nana near me. I turned round and there she was, sitting on the couch. She was wearing her favourite Harris Tweed coat and matching hat. No walking sticks!! She was looking at me with so much love, it took my breath away. Standing on her left side was a tall figure dressed in a black hooded robe. He was extremely tall and the robe actually touched the floor. I couldn't see a face but I instantly knew this was my

Mother's Guardian Angel. I said "Oh my God, Jack, Nana's here" and with that, they floated up and drifted out of the door. I just felt so wonderful, I was so happy for her. I rushed to the door to see if they were in the hall, but they had gone. Nana had come back to see me and let me know that she was okay.

Jack said "This has been the most amazing day and I think we should make an early night of it" "You go and make the food and I'll go upstairs to the blue bedroom, switch on the heating and the electric blanket and then we'll have something to eat and a cup of tea and get off to bed"

Jack came into the kitchen and said "Do you know, the strangest thing happened, there was a butterfly in the bedroom!!" I almost fainted, "where is she? What did you do with her?" "What do you mean her!" said Jack. "Nana! Where is she?" I yelled.

He said "I opened the window and let it out" "Oh my God! You put Nana out in the cold with all that frost and snow! How could you??" " Now just hold on", said Jack calmly. I don't know what this is all about but I've let her spirit fly out, she is now free!!" I was so happy, I felt as if I wasn't mourning any more. She had come back as a butterfly. My darling Mum had let us know that she was safe and had crossed over to a beautiful place.

Three

---◆---

Viewing the villa

The decision to leave our beloved Brora was finally made when after a particularly stormy night the sea overflowed right up to the front door. We felt scared to stay there. It was only a matter of time before the house was flooded. Now was the time to house hunt in Spain.

We managed to sell our house quickly. Neither of us wanted to live on the coast again in view of the threat of rising seas. We contacted an Estate Agent and flew to Spain to view several properties in some of the inland mountainous areas. After an exhausting few days of viewing properties, we found a magnificent five bedroom villa encased in three huge terraces, on a mountain above the village of Muro de Alcoy in the Sierra Mariolas in Alicante state. This was in the Spanish National Park where wild life is protected. As we drove up the twisting mountain road, Jack and I looked at one another and said simultaneously "I feel we have been here before" When we drove into the grounds, again we had the "I've been here before feeling". We were enthralled by the beauty of the villa and the views over mountains, lakes and white villages. It was spectacular.

The vendors welcomed us warmly and after viewing the house, huge garden complete with granny flat and six almond and olive groves we made the momentous decision that this would be our new home in Spain.

We sat down with the vendors and the Estate agent to have coffee on the front terrace. The strangest thing happened. I heard my mother's voice say very clearly

" Get up and look at the view" (my mother had died five years before). I got up and walked over to the garden fence, looked over the edge, down the mountain and suddenly felt my mother standing behind me. She slipped her arms around my waist, just as she had done so many times when I was a child. I could feel her give me a hug and then the sensation passed. I was so overwhelmed, I burst into tears.

I turned round to see everyone watching me. Jack came over quickly and asked why I was crying. "Nana's just hugged me and I know it's good for us to be here"

"Okay" he said, "Let's buy it," and the decision was made to settle in Spain.

When we were looking over the property, I noticed several cats in various places around the garden. I explained to the vendors that we had two dogs that had never been in contact with cats so could they please make sure that none were left when they moved out.

Four

It was four months later when we moved to Spain. I made sure that the dogs had all their papers, passports, inoculations etc., and bought two large crates on wheels with pull handles, suitable for flying. We would have to break our journey at Gatwick. I made arrangements with British Air and paid a large sum of money for the dogs to be taken to kennels for the eight hours between connections. There, they would be walked, fed and watered, then returned to the airport to be put on our flight to Spain.

We landed at Gatwick, where we had made arrangements to meet Jack's son Val in the airport café, then go to meet his wife and our grandchildren and all go for lunch together.

As we were walking towards the exit, I noticed two dog crates just like ours, lying unattended in a corner of the airport. I said to Jack, "Look, somebody else has got crates like ours. Oh! My God, they are ours!" We rushed over and yes! It was Megan and Puffin. I could not believe this. We had paid almost two thousand pounds to have our dogs transported responsibly and safely to Spain and here they were just dumped in a corner, where anyone could have walked off with them.

They were so pleased to see us. I took them out and walked over to the café and bought a big bottle of water.

As it happened, I still had their collapsible water dish in my hand luggage. They were so thirsty.

I went over to the BA desk to complain and was given a huge complaint form which would have taken me some considerable to fill out. I asked for a sheet of paper and wrote out a formal complaint to BA which the girl accepted and said if I wanted anything done about my complaint I would have to fill out the form. I said I would do this later and post it to them. I did this when we arrived in Spain but my complaint was ignored, I have not yet received an apology or refund of our money. At the time, I was just too exhausted to pursue the matter any further.

With the problem of the dogs, we could not now go for our lunch and made do with sandwiches and orange juice. I did manage to take the dogs outside the airport to relieve themselves and give them a walk. Then it was back to waiting several hours for our next flight.

When we checked in for our flight to Alicante, I told them what had happened with the dogs. The checkout girl called for an attendant and the dogs were taken round to the rear area and disappeared from our view. I just prayed that they would be on the same flight as us. I have lost all faith in BA's dog care service.

The dogs arrived safely but unfortunately, both of their crates had a wheel missing. I suspected that they had been removed for the flight and not put safely in the wheel storage box in the top of the crates. There was no way we could pull the crates with three wheels. I took the dogs out and put their harnesses and leads on.

I found two large trolleys and balanced the crates on top of the luggage

I had previously booked a hire car at the airport, big enough to take all the luggage, crates, dogs and Jack and I. Jack waited with the dogs while I went to collect the car keys.

The receptionist handed me the keys along with the details of the car in a folder. She said it was red and I would find it in alley G near the entrance to the car park. I was looking for a large estate car and couldn't find one anywhere. I went back to the office. "I can't find the estate car anywhere" "Oh! It's not an estate car; it's a red Peugeot 107." I said, "I ordered and paid for a big estate car" "Oh! So sorry, we didn't have any big cars left" "and how am I going to put two large dog crates, four suitcases, two dogs and two hand luggages in that little thing?"

"Oh I'm so sorry but there is nothing I can do about it, we don't have any other cars available" It was just after midnight and I was tired, angry, disgusted, frustrated and furious all at the same time.

I said, OK you're going to hear more about this and I rushed out of the door banging it hard behind me.

I had made arrangements for the estate agent to meet us at the airport to guide us from Alicante to Muro de Alcoy. I knew I would be so tired I would be unable to find our new house in the dark. I ran back to Jack and the dogs and all the luggage and crates and burst into tears. "Its okay" said Jack "the rep from the estate agent has arrived and she has a big 4x4. I could have hugged the lady. She began piling everything into her car including the crates, which we had to dismantle; fortunately they could be halved in size once the screws were removed.

I collected the Peugeot 107, put the dogs in the back seat and fixed their car harnesses securely. It took another hour to drive, home to our new home in Muro de Alcoy.

The final part of the journey was up a twisting curving mountain road. Thank goodness I had hired the estate agent; I would have been hopelessly lost.

The agent had the key for the gate and we thankfully drove in and let the dogs out to explore their new garden.

The agent also had the keys for the house, unfortunately, they didn't fit the door!

I sat down on the step with my head in my hands and prayed for a miracle. This couldn't be happening. It was now almost 3am. The agent had the telephone number of the vendors and managed to contact them. They arrived within half an hour and we entered our new home. The vendors brought a kettle, some cups, tea bags, teaspoons and some biscuits.

They made a cup of tea for all of us and we sat on the steps outside and thoroughly enjoyed it. I fed and watered the dogs.

Our furniture was due to arrive in the morning and fortunately the vendors had left a double bed, some sheets and a blanket. After they and the agent left, we all, including the dogs, piled onto the bed fully clothed and crashed out for the remainder of the night.

Five

---◆---

We all slept until 10am. The dogs had a wonderful time exploring the gardens while I made some tea and fixed cereal for breakfast.

We were looking forward to our furniture and possessions arriving from Scotland this morning. A small van arrived at the gate and the driver rang the bell. I opened the gate and he drove in. I recognized him as one of the removal men who had filled the furniture van in Brora. "So Sorry, the furniture van has broken down in France, I've driven all night to get here because we couldn't find your mobile phone number" He had one or two of our boxes in the van which he thought may be useful but it would be another three days before the big van could be repaired and our possessions delivered. What a disappointment but there was nothing we could do but wait. His company offered to put us up in a hotel meanwhile but we refused, we could not leave the dogs on their own. I made him a cup of coffee and hoped he would have a safe journey back to France.

We all piled into the car (dogs included) and drove down the mountain to Muro de Alcoy to the local supermarket. On the way we stopped at the garage for diesel and met a lovely Scottish lady who asked us if we were new to Muro. We chatted for a while and explained how we had just arrived and the saga of our possessions. Her name was Isa. She and her husband Brian were rushing off to Alicante airport to meet a friend but she took the time to point us in the right direction for the Super Mercado (supermarket). We exchanged telephone numbers and went our separate ways. Isa telephoned me later that same evening and from then on we became firm friends and remain so today.

Our first trip round the supermarket was exciting. I bought a deep frying pan which I could use for all my cooking in the short term and some everyday essential groceries, some milk, fruit and tins of dog meat. I had packed a large box of dog meat but it was stuck in the big van in France.

As we drove back up the mountain I noticed a Siamese cat sitting near our gate.

I drove in and it was then I noticed, FOUR CATS all sitting in various positions along the terrace wall Puffin and Megan raced out of the car and dashed along the terrace, cats flying in all directions. I looked towards the gate and ambling up the drive was the Siamese cat. Now there were FIVE CATS.

I did not want to have the worry of looking after all these cats and particularly as I had asked the vendors not to leave them, I telephoned them immediately to come and take all the cats away. They arrived very shortly and apologetically, bundled those they could catch, into their car. The rest, they promised to come back for later and entice them with food. Later in the evening all of the cats were rounded up and taken away from the house and grounds. I breathed a sigh of relief and waved them goodbye as they were driven away.

Three days later I noticed two of the cats had returned. They obviously preferred living at El-Pinar. On the fourth day, all of the cats were back. I telephoned the vendors and they appeared again with a large bag of cat food. We all agreed that the cats could stay but if there were any vet bills to be paid, the vendors would be prepared to settle them. Puffin and Megan would just have to get used to having another five members in our family. Fortunately all of the cats were spayed or castrated. They had been cared for responsibly.

Six

───── ◆ ─────

We had never owned a swimming pool before and this was going to be a new adventure. The pool was empty and clean, all except for some leaves on the bottom. Jack swept these up and we were ready to investigate the pump house.

This was through a gate, down a few steps into a lower grove. It looked rather complicated with lots of switches, pipes and a tool rack. The vendors had left instructions but unfortunately they were in Spanish. I couldn't use my computer to translate because it was still in the van and as yet my Spanish was not fluent enough, although I had been having lessons for a couple of months. I called the vendors again and asked if they could help out. Within ten minutes they arrived complete with pump engineer and set everything in motion. The pool was filling slowly, (this could take twelve hours). It was then that they told us that our water was on a meter. A lot of water!!

The sun heated the water which was a big saving. We could use it the next day and I should remember to switch the water off at night. Jack remembered this and we were not faced with an overflowing pool in the morning.

The dogs were so happy, jumping in and out, they didn't care that it wasn't full and the temperature was only twenty degrees. They were used to swimming in the sea at Brora in all weathers. On winter days they would come back from their walks along the shore with icicles hanging from their legs and tummies. This was a dog's life!! Jack sat on one of the deck chairs constantly throwing a tennis ball Puffin had found in the groves, while they ran round the pool sides and splashed into the water.

We had six groves of olives, walnuts, almonds, pineapples and herbs. The dogs came back from their walks smelling like herb cushions as they rushed around amongst the vast variety of herbs. The vendors had also been market gardeners and grew a variety of Mints, Nasturtium, Oregano, Parsley, Rosemary and Sage, Sorrell, Tarragon, Thyme and Sweet Marjoram, Lemon Balm, Verbena and Lavender, Lemon Grass, Fennel, Garlic, Dill, Chives and Catnip, Borage, Basil and Bay Laurel trees. The perfumes were unbelievable. I was dizzy with the perfumes. I am vegetarian and use a lot of herbs in my cooking. I would never need to buy herbs again. There was also a kitchen garden in the grove above the house, full of herbs and other goodies, so I didn't need to walk down to the lower groves every time I needed fresh herbs.

The house was surrounded by flowers and shrubs of many varieties. The summer kitchen, at the end of the end terrace, was bordered by vines hanging with grapes from the roof and the adjoining bower. This was heaven on earth.

21

We had our first swim the next morning, it was still a bit chilly because the sun had not been on the water for a full day but this was absolute luxury. Our own swimming pool!! I was surprised that Jack was staying at the shallow end and not venturing away from the sides. He said he felt a bit unsafe because he hadn't swam since last time we were in India which was two years previously. I sometimes think back and wonder if this was the start of all his illness.

I swam for fifty lengths while the dogs followed alongside. I was going to be Mrs.Keepfit from now on. I would do this every morning!

I turned on the poolside shower and rinsed the dogs, they loved this. Megan lay on her back underneath while the shower tickled her tummy. This was also a doggy heaven.

Every day the pool had to be cleaned. I bought a little pool robot which was christened Robbie. He would wander all over the pool floor sucking up all the debris blown by the wind and dozens of tarantula spiders who committed suicide during the night, thank goodness.

Seven

---◆◆◆---

I started to notice a change in Jack shortly after we arrived in Spain. He showed a reluctance to help out in the groves, which was one of the things that he had been really excited about.

We were now registered as Spanish Farmers. The groves on our property were centuries old and had always been farmed by local people. Most of the olive trees were aged from one to three hundred years. The almond trees were also ancient. All had been meticulously pruned and harvested with so much care and attention to their welfare. The groves were completely free of weeds and the fruit was bulging on the trees. Olives can be harvested from November to March depending on the weather. We started picking them in December. We first picked the olives which had fallen on the ground. They were collected and put into separate baskets. They could still be pressed but were considered inferior, damaged fruit and couldn't be marketed as extra virgin oil.

We spread large nets under the trees and used big toothed combs to strip the olives off the individual branches. These were then collected up in the nets and poured into straw baskets then tipped into sacks and taken to the Almazara (the pressing mill) for processing into the highest quality extra virgin olive oil. The crop must be processed the same day it is picked. We bundled the sacks into the boot of our estate car and I drove them down to the pressing mill where we were paid by the weight of the olives. We could also wait while it was hot processed and take some flagons of our very own olive oil for personal use. We were both excited.

Our Spanish neighbours came to help and when we were hungry, we all sat in the groves at a long wooden table and lunched on home made bread and cheese, garden tomatoes and freshly picked oranges and local wine. What a thrill !!

The same thing happened when it was time to pick the almonds but these were harvested differently. After spreading the nets, the branches were hit with long poles to knock the nuts off the trees. They were still attached to their furry outer shells and these had to be separated after they were transported back to the terraces bordering the house. We had a huge marble table on the side terrace and we all sat round this, cleaning the nuts, chatting, sipping cups of tea, glasses of wine, sandwiches and cheese. We absolutely loved these times with friends and neighbours.

Jack's disinterest in the harvests started early on and although he did relish hitting the trees with the poles, he had no interest in shelling the fruit but did enjoy the company of our friends. He had reached the stage where he could not bear to see me out of his sight. He was nervous and afraid if I left him.

Eight

It was around this time that he began to lose his temper a lot. Little niggling things would loom very large and he would make a mountain out of a molehill at the slightest excuse. He forgot how to shower himself and kept falling over. He constantly asked me to help him shave and comb his hair. He had always been so totally in control.

At dinnertime Jack asked for more rice. I said there was no more and he could fill up with his dessert. I could see his face get very red and he flew into a temper, shouting and yelling at the top of his voice. Calling me horrible names and I wasn't fit to be living in his house and I should get out now or he would hit me with his stick.

I managed to wrestle his stick out of his hands and threw it outside. He walked over to the phone to make a phone call, tried to sit down on the chair and fell off the side onto the floor. I tried to help him up and he yelled as loud as he could that I was beating him up. He grabbed my wrist and twisted it. He broke my gold bracelet which had just been repaired by the local jeweller. One of the ivory figurines fell off the sideboard and smashed in three pieces. He also broke a picture frame and continued to yell at the top of his voice while coming towards me menacingly. He was like a wild animal. I pushed him back and he caught me across the top of my arm, which was later covered in a black bruise. I managed to push him on to the couch and rushed outside, shutting the door behind me. I could not believe what had just happened. He was like a wild animal. I was in a state of shock and shaking like a leaf. In all of our marriage, I had never heard Jack swear or use such obscenities. I had trusted him implicitly; he would never have lifted a finger to harm me.

He didn't follow me outside and I sat on the terrace to try to get over the state I was in. I waited about ten minutes and ventured back into the lounge. He was sitting on the couch with his head in his hands. He suddenly relaxed and started to cry.

"Oh God! I'm so sorry, what happened? I love you; I didn't mean to hit you."

I was still shocked and couldn't reply. I was still shaking all over and tears were streaming down my face.

Puffin and Megan had fled out on to the terrace and were cowering under the marble table. The cats had disappeared. None of them had ever witnessed violence before. At that present moment I just wanted to go away and hide myself. This was domestic cruelty and I had to make sure it didn't happen again. I sat outside on the terrace, I cried for a long time. I couldn't stand to be anywhere near him.

I didn't reply. He eventually appeared round the corner of the terrace and came over to me. He sat down beside me and put his arms round me. He also was crying. I asked him why he was crying and he replied "I can't remember!!" He appeared to have completely forgotten what had just happened.

Nine

I telephoned the surgery and made an appointment with our doctor for first thing the next morning.

I told her what had happened. She gave Jack a complete examination, checking his heart, pulse, blood pressure etc., and said she would make appointments for him to see the neurologist and a psychiatrist at the hospital in Alcoy. She said appointments would be sent as soon as possible. To my utter surprise, the hospital called me two days later and said appointments had been made for the following day and I would see both consultants in the afternoon. How was that for service??

The neurologist asked many questions relating to his moods; did he forget where he put things? Did he put things in peculiar places? I said he had on a couple of occasions, put his slippers in the fridge and put his straw sun hat in the dog's cupboard. Jack was unable to answer any of her questions sensibly. He just could not remember and would stop half way through a sentence and ask what he had been talking about. This was worse than I thought. She asked if he had ever had any head injury in the past. I told her that Jack had a bad accident in India around thirty years previously. He had been riding his motorcycle and was hooked by the arm with a passing lorry. It dragged him quite a way until the driver noticed people shouting. He suffered severe head injuries and had been in a coma for several weeks. When he came to, he could not remember a thing about the accident. He returned to normal fairly quickly with the help of the best medical treatment money could buy. Jack's father was a lawyer and the cost was not a problem.

The information I had given was passed over to the Psychiatrist and then we spent another hour being questioned about many different things and Jack would be called for a brain scan before the end of the week.

The brain scan was done on Friday, all of this happened within a week.

We were given an appointment for the following Tuesday and we were told the shocking news that both specialists were almost sure that Jack had Altzeimers Disease. I was filled with doubt but had no alternative but to go with the decision they had made.

Almost immediately, plans were being made for home nursing and day care services. He was given a place at the Day Care centre in Muro de Alcoy, ten minutes from our house. He would go there from nine in the morning until four in the afternoon. He would be given his morning coffee, lunch, have his siesta after lunch and then afternoon coffee or juice before I collected him at four. These services were provided for Euros 40 per week. Amazing!!

Jack's nurse arrived one week later. Esther, an absolutely lovely young Spanish lady. She came every morning at eight o'clock for one hour. She showered, shaved and dressed Jack, prepared his breakfast, gave him his medication and insulin and then took him down to the day care centre. The cost for nursing service was also Euros 40 per week. This was just wonderful.

Jack was not too happy about the day care but I convinced him it would make a difference to his life style and I could also have a rest. I had been caring for him twenty four hours a day. I was wary of having him out of my sight. I was unsure what his next move would be.

Ten

O ur lovely neighbours, Jenny and Ian had also retired to Spain and lived two hundred yards down the road. I was working in the lower groves, weeding the herb plots when Jack came to the fence and looked down.

"Come up here now, I'm hungry, come and make the food" he called.

I told him I was busy and would be up in half an hour. I asked him to start making the dinner and to please set the table on the front terrace.

I continued working until I had finished the Thyme and Rosemary then wandered up to the villa to see how Jack was getting on.

He was nowhere to be seen, neither were the dogs!

The phone rang, it was Jenny calling to say that jack was down with them and was complaining that he was starving and I was neglecting him. He had also taken the dogs without their leads. I told Jenny I would be right down. I met them all coming up the road, dogs on the loose and Jack holding on to Jenny's arm. She had decided to accompany him just to make sure he was safe. I gave them both a welcome hug and invited Jenny up for a coffee. Jack was rather rude to Jenny and told her there was no need to come, we could manage without her. I am always horrified by the angry things Jack comes out with and keep apologizing. I frequently tell him "Now, now, put your angry monsters back in the cupboard and be the gentle gentleman you should be."

This usually brought him back to an even keel, but not always.

Jenny stayed to have coffee with us and Jack had returned to being a good host by the time she left. She is a lovely lady and a very good friend. It was because of our friends and neighbours that I could cope with Jack's bad Altzi behaviour. That was what we called his tantrums. I thanked Jenny and assured her that I would do my best not to neglect and starve Jack again (tongue in cheek!)

I now felt it would be necessary to lock the gate at all times and keep the key in my pocket to prevent Jack wandering off again.

Our other neighbours and friends, Ginny and Mike further up the mountain only used their property as a holiday home and visited three or four times a year. We kept an eye of their house when it was vacant. We all had the fear that it was just a matter of time before our beautiful mountain villas would be broken into one day. This was happening all the time in Spain and the police were turning a blind eye. They blamed most of the burglaries on Romanian immigrants, who did this for a living.

It was late in the evening and getting dark. I took the dogs down to the pool house to check that the pump was off. They started barking and looking up at Ginny and Mike's house. I saw a flash of light and heard a door shut. I went inside to get my big flashlight, came back to the pool and shone it up at the house.

I saw a man with an armful of clothes pass quickly from the front door to the driveway. I could see another light moving inside the house. I yelled at them "Sal de ahí, voy a llamar a la policía" (Get out of there. I will call the police.) I heard feet running, then a car door slammed and a car raced down the road.

I was a bit frightened to go up there by myself at night so I took the dogs inside and locked all the doors. Jack was already asleep.

I called Ginny and Mike with the bad news. Mike said he would come out as soon as he could get a flight.

I called the police and they sounded disinterested and would send someone up in the morning.

I didn't sleep much and kept wakening, imagining I could hear noises outside the house and maybe someone was trying to break in. It's at times like this that I miss Jack's support.

In the morning, I went up to Ginny and Mike's house. The first thing I saw was the lounge window torn from the wall and the rejas de seguridad (iron window bars) lying on the ground, curtains blowing in the wind.

The front door was half open. Inside, drawers were pulled open and things strewn around.

The kitchen was a bit of a mess with every cupboard opened, drawers pulled out and things lying on the floor.

Upstairs was the same, wardrobes and drawers opened, a pile of clothes lying on the bed obviously ready to take.

Downstairs on the lounge sofa I found a clear footprint. I photographed it.

The police arrived and I showed them around.

They said it was good I had disturbed them or they would have taken more.

I showed them the footprint on the sofa but they just ignored it. They did not take fingerprints or take pictures. I asked them why. "Oh! It's the same people every time, we will catch them. There were a lot of houses broken into last night."

I had a feeling it was a situation similar to one we experienced in India where we were told that the police were actually involved in the robberies and were taking their cut of the spoils. Police in India and Spain are very poorly paid. Perhaps it was the same here.

Eleven

The following week I drove Jack down to the Salud for his health check. I noticed a red car tailgating me the whole way down; it was so close when I drove down the main street, I thought it would run into the back of the car. I was getting really mad and when I reached the turn in to the salud, I slammed on my brakes and the red car veered sharply to avoid me and hit another car on the side of the road.

I drove off and a man jumped out of the red car. He ran along the road following me. I reached the salud and the man just walked quickly past my car and carried on up the road. He disappeared round the bend. I didn't go back to see what was happening with the red car because we would have been late for Jack's appointment and in Spain if you are late, you just go to the back of the queue and could be sitting there all morning waiting to see the doctor.

I got Jack out of the car and we went into the surgery, thank goodness, we were just on time. In my rush I had forgotten to take Jack's medical records from the car. In Spain, patients look after their own records.

I went back down and rushed over to open the car door. On the other side was the man who had followed me to the salud. He had a phone pressed to his ear.

I asked him what he was doing and he turned and walked off.

After Jack was finished in the salud, we got back in the car and drove home.

As we were driving up the hill, I pulled in to let a dark maroon Nissan saloon pass me. I suddenly had the horrible feeling that our house had been broken into.

I opened the gate and thought, Oh! Thank goodness, the gate is okay, they didn't get in. I wondered where the dogs were, they always come to meet us with tails wagging. They were nowhere to be seen.

I opened the door and the first thing I saw was our little red cash box lying smashed on the floor, passports and personal papers spread around. I wondered how on earth they had fallen there. I walked along the hall and found absolute disaster. All the cupboard doors had been torn off the hinges (why did they do that? They could just have opened the doors) the safe cupboard was smashed to pieces but the safe was still intact and unmoved. Rubble and costume jewelry items were scattered everywhere. Hundreds of books had been deliberately thrown on the floor from the book shelves.

It suddenly dawned on me that I was right about the maroon car. The man at the salud had been phoning the robbers to say we had come out and were on our way back.

I went through to our bedroom and it was in chaos also. The dressing table was upside down, the bed was littered with empty jewelry boxes. (All my beautiful presents I had been given for my seventieth birthday a few days before.)

The big wood axe, which Camilo had not put away in the garden shed, was left beside the car port and they had used it to smash through the bedroom wall into the back of the safe cupboard. They could not get in from the front so they tried from the back.

They had actually tried to bash out the back of the safe and succeeded in only denting it.

I take personal pride in the fact that I fitted the safe and did a good job. I had bolted it through the concrete floor and also into the wall at the back.

They had obviously rushed out of the back door because they knew we were coming.

I walked through to my office. I first noticed the window. It had been smashed out and the rejas forced with a crowbar from the wall. It looked as if they had used the axe for this also. The rejas were pulled back against the outside wall and the mess was just breathtaking. They had hacked huge holes in the four anchor places to get out the iron. They had obviously come in that window because my printer was on a desk underneath and had been smashed where they stood on it. Every cupboard and drawer was thrown open, some were smashed, and the contents were everywhere. A lot of articles had been taken including my computer, Jack's laptop, cameras, video camera; even the phone had been pulled from the socket. My handcraft cupboard had been emptied and all the contents of individual boxes were indiscriminately scattered everywhere. Thousands of small beads, jewelry making equipment, my art brushes, pallets and paint boxes were smashed; I could see heel marks where they had trampled on them.

I just stood there in a state of shock. I don't know how long I was rooted to the spot. Jack came up behind me and wrapped his arms around me.

"Never mind darling, it's only material things" He wasn't even angry.

It was then that I remembered the dogs. Where on earth were they? I was shivering with terror. I called their names, but no response. I rushed outside and found Puffin wandering around by the pool. He was deaf and almost blind and was in a confused state. Thank God he hadn't fallen in. I noticed that he was dragging his leg. He had obviously been kicked. I ran over to him and cuddled him. He was so pleased to see me, he was wagging his tail ecstatically. I told Jack to stay there and fetched one of the pool chairs. He consoled Puffin while I looked for Megan. I ran up to the granny flat at the end of the garden but she wasn't there. Then I heard a whimper. There she was in the old concrete dog kennel. She was terrified. She came out when I called her but her belly was touching the ground and she was crawling towards me. She was so traumatized. I sat down on the ground and she laid her head on my lap. I cuddled her and spoke to her gently "my poor little girl, what have they done to you?" I felt her all over and she squealed when I touched her left side. I sat there for a long time stroking her head to comfort her. If I could have caught those evil devils I would cheerfully have stabbed them.

In the afternoon I had Puffin and Megan checked over by the vet in the village, Almu was on holiday. He said it looked as if they had been kicked.

I can imagine how protective they would have been and both would have tried to prevent these robbers from touching our home.

Megan was the worst affected, she hid under the dining table and wouldn't even come out for her dinner. She really was spooked. When the electrician was putting the new spot light at the back of the house and started hammering the wall, she fled to the other end of the house and hid under one of the li-los. They were both suffering from severe shock. How I hate these men!

I believe in karma and I know that these people will at some time in their vicious, lives be made to feel the distress, hurt and sense of loss they have inflicted on so many innocent people.

Jack and I could not sleep properly for ages. We kept waking up to talk about the robbery. It was not only the dogs who had been spooked.

The insurance agent said that the robbers were a regimented, organized gang of crooks. They are

Romanians who had come over to Spain to make a living by stealing. More than fifty houses and flats had been robbed in Muro de Alcoy over the last week. The police seemed powerless to stop them. The gang had so many lookouts watching the houses to see when people go out.

The fabric factory at the bottom of the road had also been broken into and a huge amount of things stolen during the night. The world famous Alhambra Guitar Factory is in Muro and it also was badly damaged. The police said the robbers shut off the alarms using their mobile phones. (I wonder how they did that ??)

The police said they knew they had lookouts at all four corners of the buildings because they were all eating pipas (sunflower seeds) and dropped the shells. Great detection!!! They entered the houses and used metal detectors to find the valuables. They knew exactly where to go. I wondered why they had to smash our house to bits, if they knew where to go!! I suspected it was because I had surprised them at Ginny and Mike's house, we got an extra beating!

The insurance agent said he thought they wouldn't come back for two years at least, but they certainly would be back. This was their livelihood.

In the morning, Katia (our cleaner) came and I felt brave enough to leave the house. I left Jack at home, I told him it was his job to look after the dogs. I went to the Farmacia (chemist) to collect some prescriptions and Elia, who owned the business with her brother, told me that her assistant chemist, who lived at the very top of our road, was also robbed. Then a new customer who lived in an apartment down the street came in and said she had been burgled. That was three of us, at the same time. How many other poor souls have been affected?

I personally felt I could no longer live comfortably in Spain. I was scared to go out incase they would break in again. These disgusting men have a lot to answer for!!

I called the insurance company and a rep came out within half an hour. He photographed all the damage and said he would send some tradesmen to repair make repairs. He asked me to write a list of the stolen goods.

It was a mammoth task, the whole house had been trashed, even the kitchen cupboards had been ransacked. I noticed that a plate of sultana cinnamon pancakes I cooked in the morning had been almost finished. I hoped they would choke on them.

The carpenters arrived in the afternoon and repaired the doors, cupboards and drawers. They could not repair the damage to the safe. It had to be replaced.

I was surprised at how quickly they worked and everything was done perfectly. I could now start putting things back in place.

Friends arrived to help clear up. I never cease to be amazed at the kindness of people. They just rolled up their sleeves and within a few hours everything was back in place and we were sitting out on the terrace enjoying a glass of wine.

The glazier arrived from the village and changed the double glazed windows. It was not so easy with the rejas because they had to be specially made but the builder promised they would be ready by the next day.

He arrived next morning and fitted the new rejas. He must have worked late into the night to get them ready.

All of the tradesmen were extremely helpful and did a great job.

I sent a list of all the things that I thought had been taken and this came to a sizeable sum. The insurance company paid us a minimal sum of Euros1800 for my jewelry and said that was the maximum they could allow because we did not have photographs of everything. The antique box with the photos had been stolen. What a racket!!

We never did get over the feeling of fear. From the day of the robbery until we left Spain, we could not leave the house or return without dreading what may happen when we were absent.

Twelve

M ost of the time, Jack was happy just to sit in his chair and watch television, he had forgotten how to change the programmes no matter how often I explain it to him. He finds it hard to make conversation and will only answer yes or no.

I some times give him things to keep him amused. I thought it would be a good idea for him to learn how to clean shoes.

Jack was brought up in India and lived a very privileged life style. Servants were always on hand to do his bidding. His servant cleaned his shoes. He told me this when I married him and made me feel that I should carry on the practice.

I didn't waste any time putting him right on that score. If he wanted clean shoes he would have to do it himself. Needless to say Jack hardly every had clean shoes. On the odd occasion when it was really important, I did polish them but he never saw me do it. I always told him the brownies had come to the house.

I collected all the brown shoes in the house, six pairs, gave him brown shoe polish and brushes and spread newspaper on the terrace table.

I gave him a demonstration on how to put the polish on the first brush and explained that it was just used to put the polish on and the other brush with the green stud on the back was for rubbing the shoes until they were shiny.

I left him to it and went round to the summer kitchen to start cooking dinner.

About twenty minutes later I wandered back round to the terrace to see how the shoe cleaner was getting on.

He was still sitting on his chair but not polishing his shoes, he was polishing his knees. He was wearing shorts. He said a piece of polish fell on his knee so he wiped it off with the first brush. It felt nice, so he kept on polishing, first one knee then the other. There he sat with two of the shiniest brown knees I have ever seen and all the shoes lying under the table uncleaned.

He eventually did manage to master the art of shoe cleaning and spent nearly every day at some point, cleaning the shoes. Since we have come back to Scotland, when I ask him to polish the shoes, he says "I just can't remember how to do it!"

Jack used to be a wonderful chef. He would cook delicious curries, using the Indian methods, fresh spices all ground to perfection with the mortar and pestle. He would prepare all the vegetables beforehand and have his chicken or meat cut up ready to cook. He was so particular about having everything in the right place and all traces of vegetable peelings would be cleared away before the start.

I asked him if he would like to peel some potatoes and carrots for me and he readily agreed. I spread a newspaper on the table along with the bags of vegetables and the potato peeler. It was one of the modern ones with the sharp blade running across the top. "I don't want that, I want the one with the wooden handle" "Okay, I'll have a hunt and see if I can find it" I practically emptied my untidy utensil drawer and found the faithful old peeler at the back. Breathing a sigh of relief and thinking, "thank goodness I never throw anything away"

I asked him to peel six potatoes and six carrots. He started the peeling, slowly and deliberately, tongue sticking out between his lips. He was really concentrating on this.

I left him to it. I went round to the front terrace and lay down on the settee to read my book.

I woke up with Jack roaring at the top of his voice. "Where are you? I've finished the potatoes and carrots" I dragged myself up and wandered round to see the results.

Jack was sitting surrounded by potato and carrot peelings. They were piled on the table, scattered in heaps around his feet, all over his shorts and the chair. He was grinning and looking so triumphant. He had peeled every potato and every carrot, the bags were empty. "I am proud of you!!" I said, you have worked so hard. There were at least twenty of each vegetable. He was ecstatically happy. I said, "Now let's see! We'll have cream of potato and carrot soup tomorrow for lunch and then we can have tatties and milk and butter for tea. Then on Tuesday we can have potato and veg curry. What do you think we can have for dinner on Wednesday?" He replied "fish and chips!!" We both had a good laugh and I gave him the brush and dustpan to sweep up the peelings which he deposited in three plastic bags.

He then took a walk down to the olive tree beside the gate and deposited them on the compost pit.

Thirteen

———◆———

It was a beautiful morning, sun shining, azure blue sky.

It was time to clean the pool area. The pool loungers needed a good scrub and after a heavy wind, there was a lot of debris to sweep up.

I was wearing shorts, a strappy top, flip flops and a wide brimmed straw hat.

I decided to move all the loungers to one area and then turn the jet hose on them.

They all had wheels so they were easy to push. I had moved two and started to move the third one. I had just slightly shifted it when I felt a sting on my ankle. I looked down and saw loads of wasps pouring out of one of the wheels. Within seconds I was being stung all over. I could just feel tiny pin pricks, one even attacked my face. I was flapping around trying to get them off and tripped over the edge of the tiles. I landed in the pool with an almighty splash, and surfaced to see my hat floating around and my flip flops at the bottom of the pool.

The wasps were still buzzing around angrily, so I just stayed put. The water cooled the stings down.

I stayed in the pool for quite some time and occasionally ducked underneath the water when one of the little blighters came near.

They had been nesting in the wheel and resented having their home disturbed.

I was furious and covered in stings; I got out of the pool and raced over to the utility area and found an insect killer spray. I barged back to the lounger and started spraying furiously. I could see the wasp bike inside the wheel; there were holes all round so it was easy to reach all sides.

I sprayed until the can was empty. These blasted wasps were not going to attack me again in a hurry.

I changed my wet clothes, got Jack into the car and drove down to the emergency department at the salud (Health Centre) and was immediately shown into a cubicle. The doctor examined all the wasp stings then injected me with antihistamine and a steroid. He said I must now be very careful not to be stung and I should carry strong antihistamine tablets with me at all times.

Jack was so concerned about me. He kept asking me all the way home if I was okay. He made me sit down on the couch and said "You sit there and I will make you a cup of coffee"

Jack hadn't made a cup of coffee for almost a year. I waited patiently and eventually he appeared with a tray holding two cups and some biscuits. The cups were half full of coffee, which was lead cold. He said," I hope you will like this, I've made iced coffee" I was so surprised, he actually had made iced coffee and it was just perfect.

Every so often a window would open and Jack would be normal again. I was always disappointed when the window closed and he had forgotten the event.

I awarded him a gold star. We always say this to each other when we have done something to be proud of.

Fourteen

———— ✦ ————

We had just come back from a walk with the dogs on the olive groves. We came through the gate and the dogs ran over to the side of the car port to stand looking down in to our neighbour's groves. They were very interested in something down there and both of their tails were between their legs, so I knew something was amiss.

To my horror, I saw one of his dogs dangling from a tree. It was shaking and twisting. The swine had hanged it. He was standing watching it. I was so angry. I screamed at Pepe, "cortarlo, cortarlo!!" ("Cut it down, cut it down") He looked up at me and laughed. "es senora normales" (it is normal senora) "ella ha terminado para la reproduccion" (she is finished breeding) then he laughed again.

I could do nothing, "you pig" I shouted.

I screamed at our dogs, "come away, come away, don't look" then ordered them back to the house. I was so angry; I was crying and moaning at the horror of what he had done to the dog.

Jack was so alarmed when he saw me in tears; he wrapped his arms around me, begging me to tell him what was wrong. I just couldn't speak, I was sobbing so hard.

Eventually, I calmed down enough to tell him. He was so upset and wanted to rush down to the neighbour's house and "shake him by the back of the neck". I managed to convince him that it would do no good and he said "God will do the same to him, he will die in fear and agony when his time comes" I had to agree with him and hope that he does suffer the same as he made that poor dog.

I reported him to the police and was told that he would be investigated. I was sure that the police would turn a blind eye, just as they did to the robberies.

About a month later I was told by our Spanish lawyer friend that all of Pepe's dogs had been taken away from him and placed in care. He had been fined Euros 6,000 and banned from keeping dogs for life. If he takes on more dogs, he will be sent to prison for six months. Hip, hip, hooray, how I hate the man, he has been punished and I am glad.

Spain is changing its attitude towards the ill-treatment of animals and the law is also becoming intolerant of animal cruelty. It used to be the accepted thing in Spain, just like India, but the Brits are pressurizing for stronger penalties.

Fifteen

———◆———

Our collection of cats continued to be fed daily. They would position themselves on various trees around the house and then all rush to the end terrace when they heard the food bag being rattled. They were all so different.

Senorita Almendra (Madam Almond) a small female tortoiseshell, Walnut was an orange tiger, Sammy, a Siamese, Tiggy, a grey tiger and Brute, a horrible bully of a grey cat who beat up all the other cats whenever he took the fancy. I love all animals but this cat was really too much. The cats all had bad scars from his punishment. He was completely ferrell and was the only one that I had not been able to get near to. We had friends from Scotland with us at the time and Fergus offered to take him away somewhere. I had gone down to the village for shopping and when I came back Fergus and the Brute had gone. He returned about an hour later with an empty cardboard box and no Brute. He had taken him about twelve kilometers away to the other side of Benniarres Lake and let him out near some trees. I was a bit worried about him but I must admit, it was a relief not to have him bullying the other cats.

A week later I was setting the breakfast table on the terrace when I heard a cat growl. There on the Yellow Mimosa tree sat Brute. He had come home!!

None of the other cats were to be seen, he had obviously scared them away.

Later in the day, Madam Almond appeared on the terrace. Her face was covered in blood and there was a huge rip in her ear. Walnut came about an hour later with a rip down the side of his nose. I was furious. Brute had to go. He was a thug and could not any more be allowed to beat up the others. I watched while Fergus enticed him into the cat crate with some biscuits and slammed the door shut. This was positively the last time he would be allowed to behave violently in our home and the removal must be final, no coming back!! Fergus was taking a trip to Alicante and Brute was going too. He was left on the outskirts near lots of houses and we had no doubt that he would survive by shear brute force and every other cat in the neighbourhood would have to learn to keep out of his way. In the next six years, he still had not found his way back to El Pinar. I wasn't sorry and neither were the other cats.

Walnut had been unwell for over a week. He was off his food and was losing weight. I took him to Almu, who did some blood tests on him and they were all clear. She asked me to seclude him in a room and watch how much he drank and try to measure it. Walnut hated being shut in anywhere. He was drinking a lot and had visibly lost more weight. I left him to rest and didn't disturb him. He moved outside to his favourite chair on the terrace. His chair was empty when I went to the terrace at night and called to him. He didn't come!

In the morning, he walked up painfully to the terrace from the car port. I picked him up and he gave a little cry of pain. I put him on a clean blanket in his basket. A few minutes later he vomited dark green slime. He was obviously very ill.

I phoned Almu. She couldn't come straight away because some workmen were removing her front door and it was impossible to leave the house. She told me to take Walnut to the surgery and she would meet me there.

I left Jack with his nurse Esther, put Walnut on a clean blanket in the cat box and drove to the surgery in Cocentaina. No one was there. Walnut was crying in pain. I sat down on the patio and took him out of the cat box. I held him in my arms for a little while and spoke gently to him, praying that he would be okay. He was very hot, he wanted to go down. I laid him on the cold tiles. I knew he was dying. He was so ill. He was frothing at the mouth and breathing very hard. Almu arrived and took Walnut into the surgery; she shaved him on his legs, his neck and his back, but could not get a blood sample. He was very dehydrated. She took him through to the operating surgery and I knew it would be the last time I saw him alive. I gave him a gentle hug and kissed him goodbye. My poor little man was dying. I drove home, hardly seeing for tears. I just went inside when the phone rang. It was Almu. She said Walnut had a burst abscess in his stomach. She had opened him up and a great deal of yellow puss came pouring out. She had to put him to sleep. He died very peacefully in the end.

I went back to the surgery with Jack to collect our beloved little pusscat. I was absolutely heart broken. I loved him so much. I wrapped him in his little blue blanket and just burst into tears. I set him on Jack's lap for the journey home and looked at his face. Tears were running down his cheeks. He also loved Walnut.

All of Walnut's pain reminded me of something which happened to me when we lived in Brora, Scotland. I had severe pains in my stomach and had suffered bad diarrhea for nearly three weeks. I had visited the doctor on several occasions and at each time was told that this was normal for a vegetarian and to take some Imodium.

I went to work as normal and very soon after my arrival, I collapsed, I fell so hard, I hit my chin on my desk and bit right through my tongue. I called my secretary and said I was leaving for the day and drove home. At one point my car went up on the bank near Dunrobin Castle because I could hardly see and was in so much pain. I stopped at the doctor's surgery in Brora and waited a while till the he could see me. When I went into his consulting room, I sat down and told him how ill I felt and his reply was. "Have you ever considered the fact that you may be a hypochondriac?" I was really shocked and replied "and have you ever considered the fact that you may be in the wrong profession?" I left the room holding my stomach and drove home in disgust. I went straight to bed. When Jack came home at lunch time, he telephoned the doctor and demanded that he come to the house immediately, which he did and arrived within ten minutes. He said

Jack should take me to the local cottage hospital in Golspie, five miles away but to come to the surgery on the way, while he wrote a letter for the doctor there. I got in the car and Jack drove me to the surgery. We actually waited there for half an hour while the doctor saw some other patients and then took his time to write a short note explaining that I was suffering from a stomach ache, possibly trapped wind. My pain was excruciating! Jack was furious. I thought he may strangle the doctor.

When we arrived at the hospital, the surgeon met us at the door. He said "My God! You look awful" and we proceeded to his consulting room, He told me to lie on the table and felt my stomach. After just a minute he said, I will have to operate on you immediately. I was put on a wheel chair and pushed into the operating room.

I was not even prepared. After I was anesthetised he opened me up immediately and after I came round he told me that when he cut into me, the puss hit him in the face. I had a burst abscess on my colon. He found my colon up under my chest.

Mr. Rosenberg saved my life. He said if I had come another half an hour later, he would not have been able to save me. I told him what my doctor had said and he was furious. I heard him say. "That idiot's head is going to roll"

My doctor did eventually apologise profusely to me.

I knew exactly the pain my little Walnut had gone through and never have forgiven myself for not getting him to Almu sooner.

I called Camilo and asked him to come over in the afternoon to dig a hole for Walnut's grave. He arrived at three o'clock with his wife Antonia and their two grand children. He dug the grave under the olive tree by the gate, where I could see it from the terrace. I kissed Walnut goodbye and laid the precious little soul in the ground. Both Puffin and Megan came over and sat beside the grave looking at the little bundle. They had also come to say their goodbyes.

I gave Camilo a sheet of wire netting to cover the grave to make sure no other animal would dig Walnut up. He laid this in the grave and filled up the remainder with earth. Then he walked over to the rose bushes and picked four roses and stuck them into the soft ground. I hoped they would take root.

Camilo, Antonia and the children all cried a little and I nearly broke my heart. Jack couldn't come to watch, he was too upset.

It was good they had brought the children, because we all went to the pool and gave Puffin and Megan a swim. How the children laughed, this was the first time they had seen dogs swim. Our sadness was gone for a while.

I gave the children ice cream while Jack dried the dogs and then Camilo, Antonia and the children said "adios" Antonia said "No one should be alone when they have lost a loved one" I was so very glad they had come.

I made a little headstone for Walnut.

"In loving memory of my darling friend Walnut"

"I will never forget you"

Sixteen

———— ◆ ————

This week was the worst in my life, I was so distressed I wrote a letter to Jack's son in Scotland but in the end, decided not to post it, but it was good to get it off my chest.

This was my letter:

Dear Russell,

Today, I have reached the end of my tether with Jack; this is positively the last cruel act I will tolerate from him.

I have just come back from Mercadona after going around in tears. I feel so miserable.

At this present moment I think Jack is the cruelest man I have ever met in my entire life.

Last week he was threatening to smash my computer, and then the televisions, then all the remote controls were being thrown about. Next he was pulling the cords out of the telephones. Every day of my life is spent looking after him, making sure that he is contented and well cared for. All I get in return when he doesn't get his own way is mental abuse. I really cannot take any more of this. I would like you to book a flight to come over here and take him back to

Scotland, where he can be under your care. I can no longer accept any responsibility for his care and wellbeing.

I suggested to him that we sell up here and move back to Scotland. His behaviour was vile. Stamping around the house, screaming abuse at me. The dogs were terrified. Megan and Puffin were hiding under the sideboard, frightened to move. Never have I witnessed such a tantrum from a grown man.

You cannot imagine the misery I am feeling at present. He has changed from being a caring loving husband into someone I don't even recognize. I don't want him in the house a day longer.

I wish your father no ill will and I know you will also not be able to suffer his outrageous behaviour. I would advise that you start making plans to have him placed in a retirement home; otherwise your life will become a living hell also.

He always appears to be happiest after he has created havoc and caused terror to me and the dogs alike. He has succeeded in pushing me over the edge. Always, he says he is sorry and it will never happen again, but it always does. His illness is the most hellish on earth. It is tearing him apart and destroying our lives.

It was a good decision not to send the letter but I always felt better if I wrote down how I was feeling. Then the hurt became a lot less and I was able to deal with it, till the next time. Between these burst of vicious behaviour, he was back to his normal loving self and would completely forget about his violent outbursts.

I was discussing all this with Michael and Joanne and they suggested that I engage an au-pair. Joanne knew of several people who would be delighted to come out to Spain and help out.

A definite decision was made and in due course Matthew arrived from Shetland. He was nineteen and taking a gap year from University. He was intelligent and an extremely likeable young man.

He had previously been studying at the University of Aberdeen and had also worked with children with learning difficulties. This was a good opportunity to work with an Altzeimers patient and add to his list of experiences. Before he left Shetland, he had read up on Altzeimers disease and had a fairly good idea of what to expect.

We drove down to Alicante to meet Matthew at the airport. It was the most stressful drive I have ever had in my life.

All the way down Jack ranted, raved and shouted at the top of his voice about not wanting a man to look after him, he didn't need anyone. He was perfectly capable of looking after himself. Matthew was not getting into the house and even supposing he had to drag him by the scruff of the neck, Matthew would be sent to stay in the granny flat. Matthew would not be allowed to lay a hand on him and he certainly would not be allowed in the house to let me go out with my friends for coffee. This went on non-stop for the complete journey.

I left Jack sitting on a chair at the arrival gate and walked up to the barrier to meet Matthew. I was just sick with worry and didn't know what I would say to the young man if Jack continued to behave badly. My stomach was churning and I felt physically sick. I didn't know how he was going to greet Matthew. He had already made up his mind that he was not going to talk to him and I was sure that the air would be blue when we entered the car. Would there be a shouting match at the arrival gate?

A tall well built extremely handsome young man walked slowly towards me, smiling. I greeted Matthew, kissed him on both cheeks and welcomed him to Spain.

"Now", I said, "come and meet Jack."

I just couldn't believe it. Jack kissed Matthew on both cheeks, gave him a big hug and said, "How nice to see you Matthew, I've been looking forward to meeting you. We'll stop and have breakfast at a nice restaurant on the way home."

(Please excuse my language), but the bugger took the feet from beneath me. I could have strangled him.

Jack was like a new person since Matthew's arrival. Happy as a sandboy. Only God knew how long it would last!!!

Anyway, thank goodness everything turned out okay and Matthew was a great help. He brought in the sticks for the log burner, washed and dried all the dishes. Cleaned the tiled floors every day, swept the terraces and also found time to sunbathe by the pool. He enjoyed taking Jack for walks on the groves. At that time Jack was using two elbow crutches and his balance was quite good. Matthew walked Megan up the mountain road every day. She had never had so many walks and jogs in her life. (Puffin just can't get up there anymore) He continued to just puddle around as elderly dogs do, enjoying the sunshine and swimming in the pool. He did manage to rush with Megan to the kitchen when the alarm went off for their meal times. His hearing was deteriorating but he kept a close eye on Megan and if she rushed off, he would follow suit and it was sure to be something exciting. Puffin always loved his food.

Jack had a few episodes of bad temper when Matthew was with us but they never seemed to last long. We both missed him when he went back to Shetland.

Seventeen

———— ◆ ————

I always said that the only problem I could foresee living in Spain was the language barrier. I had started Spanish lessons but could by no means understand what was being said to me in a rapid conversation or read the language.

I had been suffering from several urine infections and had been to the doctor on two occasions and tried two different antibiotics, both of which did not agree with me. The third time, she said I should use Rosalgin, to finally clear up any infection and she mentioned that I should use it in agua (water). I duly collected the prescription from the Farmacia and took the first packet of powder in a glass after my dinner in the evening around 7-30pm. I said to Jack, as I forced it down my throat, it was the foulest medicine I had ever tasted in my life. Within 15 minutes I was feeling very sick and started vomiting. The sickness was so severe, I knew I would need medical help. This was very serious. Jack called our friend Almu and she arrived twenty minutes later. I explained to her about the medicine I had taken and she examined the instructions in the box. Oh my God, Edna, she exclaimed, this is not for drinking, it's for the bidet, and you should have washed your fanny in it. She rushed to the hall wardrobe, grabbed my coat, helped me on with it, shoved a carrier bag and a toilet roll into my hands, ushered me to her car and tore down the road to the emergency clinic (salud) in Muro.

I spent the journey with my head in the carrier bag, heaving and puking the whole way.

At the clinic, I managed to vomit twice in the doctor's waste paper bin while the nurse stuck a needle in my backside with medicine to stop the sickness. Thank goodness for Almu, she new exactly what to do. She didn't tell the doctor that I had taken by mouth what I should have used on my other end, but managed to convince her that I had an allergy to the antibiotic. I left the salud with instructions to see the doctor next morning for a further checkup. The first thing she said to me was. "No more antibiotics for you for a while", go and buy Cranberry juice. Needless to say, the infection cleared up with the help of Rosalgin, used as per instructions. From then on I always used an interpreter for medical visits.

Eighteen

23rd November 2011
Earthquake

We had torrential rain, thunder and lightening ceaselessly for four days without stopping. I didn't worry about any flooding here because we were half way up a mountain and rainwater just ran over the edge down into the groves below.

I was sitting at the dining table looking out across the valley, still trying to sort out all the papers that the robbers had thrown around. There was a massive and I mean massive, explosion of thunder. It was like nothing I have ever heard in my life.

There was no flash before this. I was almost knocked off my chair. The whole house shook. I stood up and looked out of the front window in disbelief, I watched our fence, wall and half of the front garden, just slide away from view and disappear into our neighbours groves.

I was rooted to the spot, waiting for the house to follow the garden. I was even leaning backwards to balance myself. Thank you God, it didn't happen.

I rushed outside and looked at the destruction. Part of the wooden fence was hanging in mid air and dangling nine meters over the groves below. There was a huge crack in the ground three feet back from the edge. A large central part of the fence was lying smashed at the foot of the drop. Both sides of the fence were still intact but dangling over the drop, it was just a matter of time before they too disappeared over the edge. The drop was about nine meters. I could see roses lying around in the rubble.

We had made a memorial garden for Jack's brother John who died in India six months before and this too had gone over the edge. There was a waterfall running from the top of the drop to the bottom. Water had collected behind the wall in huge quantities and the massive explosion had cracked it and whole wall had burst open with the weight. I walked over to the remaining part of the wall where the ground was cracked and felt the ground shiver under my feet. I jumped back just in time. The rest of the wall, fence and three yards of the garden, slid slowly down into the groves. The collapse was stopped by a very old olive tree on the right side. I was yelling at the dogs to stay away and realized that Puffin couldn't hear me. He was walking towards the drop. I rushed over and grabbed his collar and pulled him back.

This was a really dangerous situation. I would have to get the area fenced off quickly. Puffin was deaf and blind.

Jack was sitting on the end terrace and quite unaware of what was happening.

I told him to come round to the front terrace to see the damage.

He said "God must have been really beating his carpets"

I telephoned our insurance company and the agent appeared within half an hour.

He had a look at the damage and checked the house over. "The house appears to be all right but I will call an architect to check it over thoroughly" He confirmed that the four days of torrential rain and the following vibration of the explosion, had caused the wall to burst. He would send a builder up in the afternoon to do an inspection and assess the cost of repair.

I was thinking that we didn't deserve any more bad luck.

The builder arrived and immediately estimated a cost of 30,000 Euros to rebuild the wall and replace the fence and departed to inform the insurance company.

The insurance agent phoned about an hour later and said they were not going to pay for the damage. The whole thing had come about because the wall was badly built in the first place. I had previously paid for a surveyor's report before insuring the house, which stated that they had inspected the wall and the grounds and everything was in order. They accepted my payment. I accepted their word in good faith that everything was fully insured. This included the house and contents, the granny flat, gardens and surrounding fences and walls and gates. We were insured for all eventualities except war and a meteor strike. With our luck, it was just a matter of time before a meteor did splat us.

There was no use arguing the point because they assured me that they would not pay for shoddy workmanship and the fact that they had accepted my money for the policy in the first place was not important.

Since this happened I have heard from lots of British and Spanish friends and read in newspapers that Spanish Insurance companies are notorious for taking the money and then backing off when a claim is made. The result is now that a lot of Spanish residents are no longer insuring their properties.

I set about getting quotes from different builders. It was important that the property was secured again as soon as possible. Lots of 'so called' builders appeared out of the woodwork, word spread like wildfire.

We had over twenty estimates over a period of a week, ranging from 6,000 to 45,000 Euros. It was unbelievable. Some of them just came in, looked over the drop and quoted a figure; one person even stepped too near the edge and fell down the slope bringing more rubble behind him. He was a bit red faced when he eventually struggled back up to the top again and stated that it would take at least 35,000 Euros to rebuild. I don't regret not having helped him up. I told him to please leave and stop wasting my time. The majority of them thought they had found a sucker to line their pockets. I was by this time getting tired of these cheats and kept hoping that someone decent would turn up with a sensible quote. Incidentally, only one of the estimators was Spanish, the rest were Brits. I checked through the estimates again, some of them written on scraps of paper, one on the back of an empty cigarette packet for Euros 23,000. I thought I would sleep on it and start looking again in the morning.

I was praying to God to help out here.

Jack had an appointment at the Salud for his diabetic and Warfarin check-ups. The appointment was early in the morning, diabetic tests are always taken while fasting and we were always eager to have our breakfast afterwards just in case of a hypo. There were several other people in front so I left him sitting on a chair while I walked round to the chemist to collect our prescriptions.

When I came back I met a couple of men outside. They said they had spoken to Jack and he told them that our wall had fallen down. I knew one of them; I had employed his wife as our daily help for some time. They were Jehovah Witnesses. He was sorry to hear that our wall had collapsed, he was a builder and would I allow him to have a look at the damage. We arranged to have him come up in the afternoon.

I went inside the Salud to collect Jack. He had already seen the nurses and was waiting patiently for me. We went to the local café and ordered café con leche and croissants. We loved sitting outside in the morning sunshine eating breakfast with the villagers and a little gang of British friends.

Denis arrived on time as arranged. He examined the damage, wrote copious notes and said he would go home and do an estimate. This could take a few days because he would have to contact suppliers for costs. I liked him immediately. He seemed so genuine and honest and he loved the dogs. That was a plus from me.

Three days later, Denis came back with his estimate. He could do the work for around 19,000 Euros. This included taking down the remainder of the old wall. I knew this was a genuine evaluation so now all I had to do was find the money.

I telephoned my son Michael in Shetland to tell him the news and that we would probably have to sell all our shares to cover the costs. His reply was "don't worry about it, something will turn up"

While I waited for the something to turn up, I started investigating all our assets and felt that we would be left with very little, only the value of our house.

I was already feeling that it would be better for us to sell up and return to Scotland.

The stress at this time was practically unbearable and I missed Jack's input so much. In the past, he would have dealt with these entire problems single handed.

I was so worried; I was living with a crunch of fear in the pit of my stomach. My mind wouldn't settle to deal with anything properly.

I heard my computer sing its little jingle to welcome an e-mail. There was one from Michael. I couldn't believe what I was reading. My dear boy was asking for my bank account number so he could deposit £20,000 to see us through the problem.

I could pay it back when I had the funds available.

I felt like the world had been lifted off my shoulders. I immediately telephoned Michael to thank him and tell him how relieved I felt. He had certainly answered my prayers.

I contacted Denis and gave him the contract to rebuild the wall.

I have never for one second regretted giving the work to him. Never in all my life have I come across someone so honest and trustworthy. He did not ask for one penny up front but pre-paid the materials himself and I refunded him when he produced the receipts. I paid him by the week for his labour. He was never late, or left early. He toiled away every day, rebuilding the wall with such precision. He had even planned it to lean slightly backwards, curved and strengthened the whole structure with pre-stressed steel rods.

It took him four weeks with the help of two apprentices to build the 30 meter long by 9 meters high wall. Then on top a 2 meter tall strong fence, cemented into the top layer of the wall. Now we were safe again. Thank you from the bottom of my heart Denis. You are a truly precious man.

Nineteen

———◆◆◆———

I was clearing up some of the debris from the earthquake at the kitchen terrace when Megan came bounding round the corner towards me. She was so excited, her tail wagging furiously. She kept coming over to my feet then running back around the corner, she did this four or five times before I got the message. She wanted me to follow her. We both rushed along the front terrace and round again to the utility terrace.

Megan darted over to the washing machine and rushed back to me, yelping and squealing. She dived over again and stuck her head in.

I looked inside and there, rocking gently on my washing at the bottom of the machine, was a little dog. He had a terrified look on his face and was trembling. His little head was shaking. His terror was so obvious. He had climbed in there to find some comfort. He must have struggled up over the debris from the collapsed wall. I spoke gently to him, "Oh poor baby, what happened to you?" I had my little camera in my pocket and took a shot of him. I really was so amazed to see this little animal. Megan was pushing me out of the way, she was so eager to get him out. I made her sit down quietly and put my hand very gingerly into the machine. I shut my eyes, thinking, "I'm going to get my fingers bitten", I pushed my hand in a bit further towards the frightened face. The little dog moved forward and I waited for the snap of teeth but instead, he laid his warm head gently on my hand and closed his eyes. Wow!!! I have never before felt such a surge of pure love. I could feel the sharp heat of it in my chest and down to my stomach. "Oh! little one! I knew in that moment that he was meant to be with us and us with him.

I lifted him gently out and held him in my arms. He cuddled in close and kept his eyes shut. I stroked him and he pressed his head into my neck. This was just perfect love. I walked back round to the kitchen terrace and placed him on the floor. I just gasped at the state of him. Never before have I seen the results of such cruelty and brutality. He was covered in cuts and bruises, his ribs and bones were sticking out over stretched skin. Starving and thirsty, looked like someone had used him as a football. He was covered in fleas and ticks, his legs were like twigs. I just sobbed; I was so angry that anyone could cause so much suffering to such a defenseless little animal.

I fetched a clean sheet and gently wrapped him up. He never took his eyes off me. I thought he was thinking "when will the beatings start?" I whispered to him "You are safe now little one, no one will ever hurt you again"

I took him into the house and phoned Almu (our friend and local vet) she told me to bring him straight down.

Jack held him in his arms while we drove down to the surgery in Cocentaina.

Almu checked him over gently. She said "He is about three months old, dehydrated and in severe shock, he may not survive until the morning." She put him on a hydration drip. I took him home in the car with the drip bottle hanging from the roof handle. I just didn't want to be parted from him. I couldn't leave him at the surgery. I knew this little boy was ours. Almu had also sprayed him to remove the fleas and ticks. It was unsafe at this time to give him anything internally.

Almu told me he was an Andalucían Podenco, a Spanish hunting dog.

I thought the perfect name would be "Zanussi", which was the make of the washing machine. I thought also it sounded like a Greek God.

I lay on the couch with him all night. Several times he woke up squealing. The poor little soul was having nightmares. I cuddled him and stroked him each time until the terror passed. Megan and Puffin also cuddled in beside us. They were very curious about the little animal Mummy was making such a fuss of.

Morning arrived and I was wakened with a little tongue licking my face. Zanussi was still with us. I unwrapped the sheet and removed the empty drip which I had strung over the curtain rail. He was looking so much better, his eyes were brighter. I called Almu to give her the good news.

I gave Megan and Puffin their breakfast and put them outside to wander in the garden, but this morning they wouldn't leave the door. They wanted to see Zanussi. I thought it wise not to let them make a fuss and maybe frighten him.

He was very shaky when I put him on the floor and staggered around for a bit. I fed him some dog meat which I had liquidized with some gravy. He ate slowly; this was completely new for him. I could not imagine what he had survived on before.

A new life had begun for Zanussi.

Twenty

---◆◆◆---

We had Zanussi for three days and Megan and Puffin accepted him so well, he was learning a lot from them. When they ran, he ran and when they lay down, he did the same. I had to tie him to a long run rope when he was in the garden because the wall had not yet been rebuilt and I was terrified he would jump the fence we had erected to stop Puffin falling down the bank. If he did that, he would fall down a drop of over twenty feet.

Our new pup was Jack's little shadow; and would hold on to his legs whenever Jacked walked around. He would pick him up and cuddle him at every opportunity. This was difficult because by this time Jack was using two elbow crutches and I was worried that Zanussi would trip him. He enjoyed all these cuddles and wanted to be picked up most of the time. I tried to discourage Jack from picking him up too much. He was unsteady on his feet and Zanussi would soon be too big for him to lift.

The cats were not too keen on Zanussi and we had to take that step by step. He was never vicious towards them and only wanted to play with these furry creatures. He learnt very soon that they were not to be chased and chewed. His ancestry was hunting to kill but a few sharp slaps of a cat's paw, complete with claws across the point of his nose, made sure that he knew how far he could go.

Jack and I were relaxing in the lounge complete with dogs spread across our knees when Madam Almond strolled across the back of the sofa, slid down between Puffin and Zanussi and lay across their heads. She was telling them, "She's my Mum and I'm the top cat." So funny!!

As far as food was concerned, Zanussi thought every bowl was for him and he had freedom of choice. Megan just adored him and was quite willing to share her food with the new arrival but not so Puffin. He would give him a snap on his nose when he poked into his dish in the morning and the lesson appeared to last all day. Puffin was just telling him to keep to his own bowl. He was teaching him the pecking order.

Zanussi would eat anything he could get in his mouth. He had a dose of the runs because he constantly pinched stuff out of the rubbish bag and pigged out on some old peanuts I had thrown on to the compost pit. Poor little boy. He had a lot to learn.

The ground was covered in fallen olives after a gale and Zanussi had a wonderful time munching them up before I could stop him. He was really poorly for a couple of days and Almu said his gut was full of olive pips.

Not to worry, they would eventually pass through him. I just had to be careful not to let him do that again.

Not an easy task. I put him on the run rope which kept him just out of reach of the trees but still allowed him the freedom to run around.

I had forgotten how much work there is with a puppy. At three months old, still having his milk teeth, he wanted to chew everything and also not yet house trained, his destructiveness was reaching a serious level. It was only a matter of time before he cut his new teeth on our big wooden elephants. He had already torn the long seat of the terrace swing to shreds and scattered the cushions in bits all over the garden. The laundry basket had been eaten and the contents left in tatters on the terrace. Megan and Puffin's beloved toys which they would carry around in their mouths and present to any guests who arrived, were unceremoniously thrown around, tossed in the air and then beheaded and the stuffing left to blow around in the garden like tumbleweed. The log pile for the winter log burner was scattered along the length of the kitchen terrace and several logs used as bones to remove Zanussi's little milk teeth. His new teeth were just showing and I dreaded to think of the damage they would bestow.

I removed the carved wooden elephants, including the carved coffee table with elephant heads and locked them in one of the spare bedrooms.

Every time we went out I shut the dogs inside the house. In the kitchen a few times but the damage by Zanussi was horrible. He ate the rug and chewed a large hole in the door. He bashed the pedal bin so hard it was dented out of shape and the lid wouldn't shut. I found my rolling pin which I had for over twenty years, absolutely mangled to bits like one of the pieces of firewood. Each time I said "naughty Zanussi, bad boy" and clapped my hands, he just rolled over in ecstasy and wagged his tail.

Megan and Puffin always looked so guilty when he was naughty it was as if they were saying "we couldn't stop him."

Enough was enough, I had to find a way out of this destruction. I put Zanussi in the car and took him down to the co-operativa in the village, this was a store which sold everything from local farm produce to home produced wine, cleaning products, farm cages and everything but the kitchen sink. The owner showed me a large dog cage which folded flat when not in use. It was big enough to cage a lion. It was perfect for Zanussi. He could be put in it when ever we went out and at night. He had already chewed legs on two of the antique dining chairs and eaten through the television cable. I was not there when he did it and it was amazing that he had not been electrocuted, but he has never gone near a cable again so far and probably won't for the rest of his life. The leather pouffe we had taken home from India was lovingly destroyed in an afternoon. The leather cover had been eaten and by that I mean swallowed, he had obviously had a lot of fun shaking the horsehair stuffing around, it was spread all over the dining area floor and the table, some of it was even on top of the sideboard.

I breathed a sigh of relief as I set up the cage in the lounge. There was plenty of room for it and it would not need to be dismantled every time. I fitted up a drinking bottle and let him try it out. He licked at the tip of the bottle for ages, all the time wagging his tail contentedly. Now he could even have a drink when he was inside.

This was Zanussi's new home. I lined the base with thick cardboard from a packing case, then a cot mattress and laid a fleece blanket on top. I spread another blanket over the cage so that he could have a comfortable dark place to call his own.

He just loved his new space. He settled down immediately and closed his eyes. He was in heaven. I didn't close the door of his cage until he got used to it. It was essential not to make him feel trapped. He would be able to come and go as he pleased during the day but night was a different thing. He would be shut in.

The difference was just amazing. He was so pleased with his new abode. He didn't tear up a thing, this was his property and it didn't need to be destroyed. I gave him a big indestructible plastic bone to keep him amused. I closed the door at bed time and expected there to be barking and whining all night but he slept like a baby until morning and was sitting there wagging his tail waiting to be let out. Not one bit of destruction. Good boy!!

Lots of praise and a titbit. Zanussi had found his own little heaven.

Twenty one

———◆———

I had engaged a joiner to do some minor repairs in the house. Mark, the odd job man kept telling me he would be here soon, he never came. I decided to take the bull by the horns. I put the shelves up by myself, mended the broken tile, re-grouted the tiles in the hall, put up the full length mirror, screwed on the keyhole covers and the only thing left to do was repair the tiles on the front steps which were broken by a falling branch in the gales. I gave myself a gold star and wandered into the lounge to show Jack. "What did you get that for?" he said.

"For doing the work that you should be doing", I replied. I was feeling a bit resentful that Jack was sitting around doing nothing while I did the things we should be sharing. He still showed no interest in anything except watching television.

I walked straight over to the television and switched it off and walked out of the room muttering "and you can get your own dinner tonight my lad" We were both giggling when Almu arrived after I had given him a gold star for being the best Telly Watcher of the Month.

Almu is our friend and local vet. She had come to give the dogs their rabies jabs.

Because my Spanish had not yet reached a high enough level, she would also help out by coming with us to important appointments to make sure we got it right. She came with us when I took Jack to see the heart specialist and when he went out of the main consulting room; Almu took the chance to read his notes. He had written that "Jack may have Parkinson's disease and further tests will be necessary". I had been thinking this for quite a while because of his shaking hands and the deterioration in his mental state, forgetfulness and insecurity. This also could be an answer to his lethargy.

Jack was taken to hospital in Valencia to have these further tests done. He was kept in for three days and the results did in fact show that he suffered from Parkinson's disease.

"Don't worry about a thing darling", said Jack, "I'll be better soon and we can get back to normal". How I wished this was true.

I now seriously started to think that the time had come for us to make plans for returning to Scotland.

Twenty two

———— ✦ ————

It had rained solidly for four days, now the sun came out after a night of horrendous gales. The garden had needed a drink so badly; everything looked green and well nourished. We had almost twenty power cuts in the last week, so I just switched off my computer and waited for the storm to pass.

On Monday, our Spanish gardener Camilo said it was going to rain and he was never wrong. He may not work for his four hours if it started. He came to the door about an hour later to say that it had started spitting so he would work at the back on pruning the pine trees. It was steady rain when I went to look for him about an hour later and guess where he was?? Up a pine tree with the electric tree saw trimming the wet branches. I yelled to him to come down out of the tree. He said estoy bien (I'm okay). I then screamed at him "get out of that tree, you idiot" all in English (or Scottish). thank God!! or he wouldn't come back if he understood me. He smiled at me and shouted down "tranquila Senora Edna, tranquila. To which I replied, "tranquila nothing, get out of that tree". I ran to the side terrace and pulled the plug out. I couldn't believe it; he started to tell me that the extension plugs were waterproof. I yelled back "tell me that when I have to climb the tree and collect a little pile of charred bones to give to your wife" "Get out of there!!" What a laugh, perfect material for a cartoon!

He eventually came down and sat on the terrace drying his hair with Megan's towel.

Madam Almond came in last night absolutely covered from head to four paws in sticky pine resin. She had obviously been rolling in the cut pine branches which Camilo had sawn and the new pine cones which I had made into a pile. The rain had stopped and she had taken the opportunity to get in there and hunt for lizards.

These are her favourite meal. I know when she's been hunting because I find little tails still wriggling on the terrace and Madam Almond licking her paws after devouring the heads and bodies of the poor little creatures. Lizards shed their tails to get away from danger.

She was pulling lumps of sticky hair out of her body and it was further sticking on her nose and paws. I set to with rubber gloves and tweezers and gradually pulled all the sticky bits off, I didn't dare use a chemical cleaner. She quite enjoyed the experience and just lay there loving it. I knew it wouldn't be long before she came back with a fresh covering of resin and more tails wriggling on the terrace.

Twenty three

———◆———

We were driving down the mountain road to Muro. I needed some bread and milk.

Jack was settled in his usual front seat, singing quietly "I want to go back to Brora" as we went.

Suddenly he shouted "I need a poo!!" "Is it a fast one or can it wait?" I asked nonchalantly. "No it can't wait, I need to go NOW!"

We were almost in Muro so I said "Okay you can go at the toilet in Mercadona"

I drove to the back door of the supermarket and went round to Jack's side to get him out. "I can't wait; I'll just do it here" "Oh my God! I said, it will only take a few minutes to get you there." "No, I have to do it here and NOW!!"

I said, "OK, just stay there and I'll rush in and get what I need, I'll be back in a minute"

I shot across the road and into the store, rushed down the alleys for milk and bread, sped to the till and waited for two other people to get served. I was dancing from foot to foot with impatience. The Spanish lady in front of me turned round and looked at me, "los baños están allá" (the toilets are over there.) "Gracias" I just smiled and stood still.

I eventually paid for my bread and milk and rushed up the stairs to the back door.

Jack was waving and smiling at me with the car window fully open. The smell was horrendous. "Come on" he said," I've done it, I need to go home and have a shower" I slid into the driving seat and took off like a bat out of hell. "Jack said, "No need to rush, I've done it now"

We both were laughing when I opened all the windows and Jack was looking at the people we passed saying, "Look, she's holding her nose" or "He's got a hanky over his mouth". All the way home we giggled and yucked at the smell. Jack was sure that everybody we passed could smell it. I always say to Jack "If you can't improve it, laugh at it" This was one of those times!

We reached the gate; I opened it and quickly drove inside. The dogs came rushing round the side of the house. I drove up to the terrace, hopped out and gave them their usual cuddles and said "right you guys, stay out of the way, Mummy's got important business" They both rushed round to Jack's side of the car with tails wagging at a fast pace. I shooed them out of the way.

"I know what I'll do Jack, you get out of the car and stand at the bottom of the steps. I'll go round to the pool and get the hose pipe and we can clean you up here." It was 34 degrees and brilliant sunshine and very private.

I helped Jack out and rushed along the terrace to the pool. I dragged the hose from the water and proceeded to haul it round the terraces. I stopped at the utility area to put on a pair of latex gloves. It was a really long hose so I didn't need to disconnect it. The water in it was warm, the pool was 28 degrees and most of the hose was lying in the sun. It probably took me about five or six minutes to get back.

Half way along the terrace, Zanussi passed me at a rate of knots with something white flashing from his mouth. He was whirling it round his head and jumping up and down. "What have you got now, you little rascal?" I continued dragging the heavy hose and had to go back once to untwist it from a lounger chair. I reached the kitchen terrace and Jack was standing bare foot, holding on to the arch wall, stripped to the waist, his trousers on the floor beside his feet. That was what Zanussi had in his mouth! Jack's dirty underpants. Megan was sitting beside the trousers licking her paws. "Oh! For God's sake! Get off there you dirty little girl, what are you doing?" "You can see what she's doing" said Jack; you won't need to feed them now!!

Zanussi appeared again in a flash and careered towards the big olive tree beside the gate. He proceeded to shake his head vigorously, all the time slapping the dirty underpants against the trunk of the tree.

Needless to say, I didn't rush after him. It was time to turn the hosepipe on Jack.

He just loved his outdoor warm hosedown and sang "I'm singing in the rain" until I had finished.

Later on when Jack was all clean and fresh again, I walked down to the olive tree and found Jack's underpants with the whole gusset eaten out. Zanussi certainly knew how to make a meal of things.

Twenty four

---◆---

Zanussi refused his dinner, which was unheard of, and wandered slowly through to the couch looking extremely miserable, with his head hanging down. He appeared to be in pain. I just knew by the look of him that I should take him down to Almu to have him checked out. I telephoned her and she said to bring him down immediately. I had an appointment at the hospital with Jack half an hour later and hoped that we would be on time.

He was shaky on his legs and I helped him into the car. I left him with Almu and she said she would X-ray him and telephone me with the result. The call came when we were still at the hospital waiting to be seen.

She had found a large dark serpent like blockage almost twelve inches (30 centimeters) long. She asked my permission to operate immediately. This was major surgery and I prayed to God that he would survive.

After Jack's appointment we hurried back to the car and drove to the surgery. Jack was so worried; he must have asked me fifty times if Zanussi was still alive and had even told the specialist about the problem.

Almu met us at the door and ushered us into the recovery room where Zanussi was now lying in a cage sound asleep. She picked up a kidney dish with what looked like a coiled up snake. She held it up and guess what?? A pair of Jack's socks!!!

Whatever will this dog swallow next? Jack doesn't even have smelly feet!!

We took Zanussi home four hours later and he promptly jumped up on the couch. He yelped as he landed. He was stitched down the length of his chest and stomach.

He slept for around two hours and then went out for his wee wee. I put his basket in the bedroom and gently led him through. He lay down, rolled over with all four legs in the air and went to sleep. I placed his basket at my side of the bed so he could feel my hand. Megan's basket was there also. She curled up beside him and gently licked his mouth. She was so happy to have him back home again.

We all slept through till morning and he was none the worse for his ordeal, wandering round the pool while Megan and I had our early morning swim. Animals have the most amazing powers of recovery.

I made sure from then on that Jack's socks were well out of reach!

Twenty five

---◆◆---

Puffin was thirteen years old and beginning to get a bit slower.

In Scotland, several years earlier he had been diagnosed with Masticatory Muscle Myositis. This was a very painful disease and meant that the muscles around his head and jaws deteriorated at an alarming pace. For some time he was really ill but with the help of the Scottish vets in Rogart and some advanced medicine, he managed to overcome his problems and was still our happy little Springer Spaniel.

He had passed all his tests to become a "Pets as therapy dog" and regularly visited nursing homes in the North of Scotland.

I took Puffin and Megan over the groves with me one morning while I picked almonds and they raised a couple of wild boars who were helping themselves to the falls. I heard the crunching before I spotted the pigs; they were huge, black and quite hairy. The dogs chased them up on to the top grove but Puffin was too tired. Megan kept going but came back when I called her. These boars can be vicious beasts and can cause a lot of damage, especially if they have piglets.

A woman on the next mountain range to ours was walking her dog when a boar came rushing out of the scrub and attacked her, it bit a great chunk out of the calf of her leg and she had to spend two weeks in hospital having skin grafts and muscle replacement. The boar killed her dog when it tried to protect her. She eventually managed to whack it across the nose with a broken branch. It took off into the trees. Fortunately she had her mobile phone and called the emergency services. We saw a helicopter hovering and then a sling appeared with a stretcher and a rescuer. She could have bled to death, poor soul, thank goodness for mobile phones. After that I always took a stick and my mobile phone when I went up the mountain.

Twenty Six

———◆———

Jack was admitted to hospital with a kidney infection. His condition was worrying. His endoscope and a biopsy on his bile duct, to check for any stones or tumours resulted in several kidney stones being traced. He was losing weight fast and the specialist said it was necessary to operate soon.

It was the festival of Moors and Christians. This is the most important event of the year in Alcoy; it is dedicated to San Jorge, a figure shrouded in ancestral traditions. Huge parades and Mock battles between Moors and Christians take place in the Valencia Region. The biggest of these festivals is in Alcoy in April.

Most of the population was wandering around in costume, even the doctors, great fun, very cheerful for the patients, the only thing was that they would have to be patient until the festivities were all over and the medical staff could get back to the serious business of healing. Only extremely serious cases were dealt with during the Moors and Christians Festival.

Jack's operation was done two days later. Several kidney stones were removed. His situation became very critical over the next few days. His kidneys and bile duct were barely functioning and there were now ulcers on his kidneys where the stones had been removed. He had lost a lot of blood during the operation and a transfusion was administered.

Matthew had gone back to Shetland and I was missing him a lot. He had been such a help with Jack and the animals.

I stayed at the hospital all night and left for home at 7am.

Aaron, the son of my friend had stayed at the house overnight to look after the dogs and cats. He was a lovely lad and I had no fears about leaving the house. My feelings were still raw after the robbery.

I felt so miserable and lonely. I was wishing that Ginny and Mike had been in their villa to keep me company. I didn't know if Jack was going to survive until the evening. I cooked breakfast, had a quick shower and put on fresh clothes, then drove back to the hospital. Aaron agreed to stay on as long as Jack was in hospital. This was great for him; he spent most of his time swimming in the pool with the dogs and they just loved him.

I spent the whole day with Jack. He was really desperately ill. The doctor in charge of the ward had told me that he may not survive until the morning. They don't mince their words in Spanish hospitals. I prayed the hardest I have ever done in my life for Jack to recover.

He had been in a coma for a couple of days. On the third he opened his eyes and actually realized I was there. It was necessary for me to be with him because he hadn't managed to master the language and was always upset when he couldn't understand what was being said to him. Most of the doctors spoke good English but not many of the nurses.

Jack is a triple graduate and mastered in languages, making the situation all the more frustrating for him. All of this knowledge has now gone to sleep inside him.

Occasionally a window would open and we could have an intelligent conversation and I had to stop myself from whooping with delight, then the window closed again and Jack was back to what was now normal for him.

There was likelihood that he would either be moved to residential care or allowed home with nurses and 24 hour a day care. The cost of this was almost 4,000 Euros a month and I wasn't sure if we could afford this on a long term basis.

I had an appointment with the social workers in the morning to discuss the financial situation. I certainly couldn't manage him on my own. I was out of my mind with worry. God alone knew what the future had in store for us.

Jack's sons Russell and Val, were arriving on the following Tuesday and could only stay for two days. It was better they see him when he had turned the corner and not in the state he was in a few days before.

I was absolutely bushed; I had been running around like a scared rabbit. On the way home from the hospital, I just managed to save a little dog from straying on to the main dual carriageway. I slammed on my brakes at the junction and crossed over the road to pick it up. It came to me at once. It was a very frightened little fawn and white terrier. I put it in the car and drove straight down to Almu to have its microchip checked. I hoped it was lucky enough to have a chip. It was a dear friendly little soul. I was sure its owner must be going mad with worry.

Almu phoned me later, it had been taken down to Alicante dog pound by the police and hopefully its owner would collect it soon. I never did hear if it had been claimed.

After Jack came round from his coma, he continued from strength to strength. He is a great fighter and has managed to recover from some horrendously dangerous illnesses. He told me that he had heard me praying for him and had seen his mother and father standing by his bedside. Both of his parents had crossed over several years ago.

He spent four more days in hospital and was allowed home at the end of the week. By the time Russell and Val arrived, he was back to his usual cheerful self and I'm sure the boys were wondering what all the fuss had been for.

Twenty seven

---◆---

Every year during July and August it was too hot to sleep indoors. I could turn on the roof fans but they eventually made the bedroom too cold and we would wake up shivering.

I asked the builder to put some big hooks into the terrace roof and moved a king size bed out on to the end terrace. This was completely private and we had a wonderful vista of the valley, lakes and mountains. I bought some huge mosquito nets and suspended them from the hooks.

One was for our bed and the net completely covered the space. The other was for the three dogs. I laid their beds side by side. Puffin, Megan and Zanussi always slept beside each other. I made sure that the wrap-over opening was in line with the front of their beds. If I told them to stay after they were settled for the night, they would sleep soundly and remain there until I opened their net in the morning. They still had the freedom to get out of the net if they wanted to. I made sure that the water dish was inside the net, just in case they were thirsty.

We all loved sleeping like this. It was so cool. The temperature dropped during the night to a comfortable 18 or 20 degrees. During the day it could reach over 30 degrees

The one problem to all this comfort was Madam Almond. She always wanted to curl up beside us and would clamber up the nets, tearing holes with her razor sharp claws as she went, yelling at me in no uncertain terms that it was time to let her in. No matter how much I tried to teach her that it was easier to come in at the flap, she spent her time convincing me that it was easier to tear holes.

I kept a little box of miniature bulldog clips beside the bed and clipped each hole to prevent the mosquitoes flying in. Then in the morning I would get out my needle and thread and stitch up all the holes, only to have to do the same the next morning. Eventually our mosquito net was peppered in repairs but I was determined that a stitch in time saves nine. She never interfered with the dogs at night but always got her own way and ended up lying flat out across my stomach. None of the other cats were remotely interested in our privacy.

One evening I was laying reading when a tiny pipistrelle bat flew onto our net.

It twisted round and round and completely trapped itself. The poor little thing was petrified. The dogs were barking and jumping up and down hysterically, trying to get through their net which was very quickly being torn to shreds. I managed to get them all out and forcibly pushed them one by one into the hall through the back door. Then I could concentrate on the little bat.

It was totally wrapped up like a little cocoon. Madam Almond was crawling slowly up the net in a tiger like stalking motion.

The bat was quite far up towards the roof and I had to run and fetch the step ladder from beside the summer kitchen. Jack just stepped out of bed, stood up and put his hand round the little creature.

I managed to grab Madam Almond as she was about to pounce and pushed her inside the hall door and slammed it shut. I rushed out to the summer kitchen again and picked up a pair of scissors. After scaling the step ladder, I cut round Jack's hand and the bat. Jack sat calmly on the bed while I carefully unwrapped the little creature, he was telling me all the time to be careful not to cut it and also "be careful it doesn't bite, you could get rabies"

By this time, it was making tiny squeaking noises and in order to get the net cut off its little sharp claws on the elbows of its wings and feet, it was necessary to partially wrap it in the bed sheet. It was a tricky job and I had to be careful not to snip its claws off as well as the net. Eventually I managed to free the little bat completely. It sat peacefully on the palm of my hand looking at me with big frightened eyes. I spoke to it. "Okay little one, you can fly free. Go and join your family." It flew off without a backward glance leaving Jack and I surrounded by tattered mosquito nets hanging like ghostly spider webs.

Twenty eight

———— ✦ ————

A couple of our friends, Jane and Martin came to the house to sit with Jack while I had a couple of hours to myself. I went down to the Chemist to collect Jack's medicines. I opened the car boot and accidentally crashed my head into the rim.

The next thing I remember is coming to, lying in the road and looking up into five concerned faces. I had such a bump and cut on my forehead, blood running down my face, but it was only a superficial cut.

They were all talking at once and shouting "llamar a la ambulancia" "call the

Ambulance." Once I got over the daze, I was okay and kindly refused any help but the chemist insisted I come inside. He very gently cleaned and dressed my wound then had his assistant bring me a cup of tea, which I greatly enjoyed and felt much calmer.

I felt such as ass. I have smacked my head on the boot lid several times but never with such force. It was just because the suction hinges are slow to raise the boot. I resolved to get the hinges repaired as soon as possible.

Anyway, nothing bad became of it except I looked like a battered housewife for about a week with blue and yellow bruising down my forehead to my eyes.

Jack took a delight in telling all our friends that he was not responsible for Edna's injuries, it was done by an old boot.

Twenty nine

---❖---

I began to notice every time we had visitors; a tortoiseshell butterfly would flutter on to the terrace and hover near to where we were sitting.

My sister Morag was visiting from New York and my friend Joan from England.

We were sitting around the big marble table having breakfast. The butterfly appeared and fluttered round our heads several times.

I said "I think that's Nana visiting us, I've seen the same butterfly so often"

Both Morag and Joan poo pooed the idea. "don't be silly" This always gets my back up, so I said, "I will hold my hand up and if the butterfly lands on my hand, will you agree that it's nana's spirit. "Yes" they both said, laughing!

I held out my hand, palm up and within a few seconds "guess what?" the butterfly landed on my hand and sat there for at least five seconds then flew off around the terrace. I was shivering with excitement. Both Morag and Joan were looking at each other in disbelief.

Morag said "You are a witch!!"

We all had a good laugh but I knew I was right and Nana was visiting us.

Always, after that day, I watched for Nana coming when we had visitors and she never let me down.

Our lovely old Springer Spaniel, Puffin was getting on in years. He was blind and deaf and I spent a lot of time making sure he was safe. He wandered around the terraces and gardens so contentedly. I had to make sure that the gate to the pool was always shut. He loved to swim but the problem was that he could no longer find his way back to the steps to get out. I used one of my grandchildren's life jackets and it fitted perfectly. I hooked his leash on to the back and he would swim round and round the pool while I walked beside him on the edge, then when it was time to come out, I steered him towards the steps.

Both Puffin and Megan used to come with me when I went for my morning swim.

They would happily swim alongside me while I did my usual fifty to one hundred lengths. How we all loved the pool.

When we first went to "El Pinar" Jack would come into the pool but as his illness progressed, he developed a fear of the water. He would sit at the side on a deck chair while we all swam but would never venture further.

I was getting worried about Puffin's heart; he was coughing a lot and seemed to be very breathless. He had been diabetic on insulin for three years. I injected him twice a day. Poor little lad, he never objected to me sticking needles in him.

I used to tie Zanussi up on a long runner rope, strung from the terrace to the big olive tree by the gate, so he could run the length of the front garden (about an acre) This gave him plenty of freedom. I heard Puffin squealing. I ran outside to find him lying on his back with Zanussi's rope tangled all over him. Zanussi was running round and round, spinning Puffin on his back as he ran. Both dogs were in a state of panic. I rushed over and released Zanussi's rope from his collar. He stood beside us as I sat on the ground and cradled Puffin on my lap, untangling the rope and talking softly to him, stroking his soft curly fur and kissing his face. He was in a state of shock. I carried him inside and laid him on the couch. I wrapped him in a sheet and sat with him until he fell asleep, my poor little old man, what a distressing thing to happen. He was now fourteen and a half. I could just imagine what he had felt.

Blind and deaf, being coiled up in a rope and spinning round and round on his back.

Almu was coming up for lunch and she checked him over. She said his heart was very bad and I should consider letting him cross over. At that time I was too shocked to even consider it. Puffin was a Pat a Pet dog. He had passed all his tests before we left Brora and regularly visited the Meadows Nursing Home in Dornoch.

When Puffin came in, all the residents in the lounge, who had been sitting gazing into space or nodding off to sleep, would suddenly become alert. Puffin is here!!

Handbags and pockets were searched for biscuits and left over sausages from breakfast. I had to ask the old ladies and gents not to be too generous or he wouldn't eat his dinner. Puffin loved his visits there and would sit down with each individual and allow them to stroke him. I loved taking him there not only because it was so good for the residents but because Nana was also resident there and Puffin was her dog, she was so proud of him.

Over the following weeks Puffin became more and more exhausted. He couldn't even walk the length of the garden. He was sleeping most of the time; had little interest in food and his life style was not good.

I telephoned Almu and said "I think the time has come to let Puffin cross the rainbow bridge" She said she would come up in the afternoon. I have had to help three of my dogs to cross over and every time, I have this guilt clawing away at me. Should I wait until he crosses over naturally or should I help him out of his pain so he can cross over to be with Nana and all our other dogs? I knew my old Labrador Rhia would be waiting for him with a waggy tail.

Almu arrived as promised. Puffin was asleep on the couch. I sat down beside him and laid his head on my lap. I cuddled him and spoke to him, even though I knew he couldn't hear me, I knew he felt me holding and loving him. His tail was wagging gently. I kissed his head and told him it was time to go to Nana and Rhia.

Almu injected him and he lifted his head to look at her, then fell back on to my lap.

Within ten seconds my little boy was gone. I was thinking of all the happy times we had together and asking God and Nana to take care of him and please make sure he could see and hear again. (Oh God!! As I am writing this the tears are coursing down my cheeks and my head is burning with grief, I still feel the pain as if it were an hour ago)

I hadn't, up until then, noticed Megan and Zanussi. They were both sitting very close to us. Megan put her front paws up on the couch and gently licked Puffin's nose, then turned and walked over to her basket. She had said goodbye. Zanussi looked into my eyes and nudged Puffin hard with his nose. I'm sure he was trying to wake him. Then he too walked over to Megan's basket and snuggled in beside her. I know they were also grieving for their sweet gentle brother.

Almu asked if I would like to have Puffin cremated. Her friend had an animal crematorium. She assured me that I would definitely get Puffin's ashes back.

They would be ready for me in a week.

A couple of days after Puffin died, my friend Gema came up for coffee. We were sitting on the front terrace. I suddenly noticed two tortoiseshell butterflies fluttering round our heads. I knew immediately that Nana had brought Puffin back to see us. I was ecstatic. I told Gema about Nana coming back as a butterfly and now Puffin also.

At the end of the week, Almu phoned to tell me that Puffin's ashes were with her in the surgery and I could come and collect them. I helped Jack into the car and drove down immediately to Cocentaina.

Almu handed me a brown paper parcel tied with string. It was the size of a chocolate box. I remember thinking "is this all that's left of my little boy?"

She gave me a hug and said she would be up later to see me.

We opened the parcel together as soon as we arrived and I had settled Jack on the couch. I unwrapped the brown paper, then two layers of bubble wrap. Inside was a beautiful little glass leaded casket with TWO BUTTERFLIES on the top. Inside the casket was a little velvet bag containing Puffin's ashes.

I had not told Almu about Nana coming back as a butterfly. I immediately called her and asked if she had seen the casket when she visited her friend. She said "no, I just left Puffin with Jose and the parcel was delivered here today.

Now I knew for certain that all our loved ones including our pets cross over to a new world.

Thirty

---◆---

Another horrendous week from my diary.

Monday

I spoke to the physiotherapists at the day care centre today and asked them to show Jack how to get up when he falls, he also needs to walk around a bit more at the centre and not sit in the one place all the time. They agreed to spend more time with him, and will make him walk and exercise.

Tuesday

Jack fell off his chair in the garden today. He fell asleep in the sun and just tipped over. The hunters were shooting bore on the groves.

I think maybe he got a fright when he heard the guns. I heard him yelling, I thought he had been shot and rushed round to the front of the house. He was lying on his face on the gravel. I managed to get him up with the help of two cushions under his knees and holding on to the seat of the chair. He looked so shocked, he had a terrified expression. His knee was grazed. He was very heavy and I hurt my back helping to get him up.

Wednesday

Jack was picking up the dog poo in the garden with the white scoops. I heard him yelling and rushed out to find him spread eagled on his back beside the fence. I used the same chair method to get him up. It was comparatively easy for him this time. I asked him where the poo box was and he said "I don't need a poo box; I just threw it down into our neighbours groves." I could only hope he hadn't seen him do it.

Thursday

Jack fell again this morning when he was trying to get to the toilet. He was rushing as usual. He was at the foot of the bed when he crashed backwards. His head hit the cupboard. He wasn't injured, but was lying on the tiled floor and couldn't get himself up. I pushed a big towel under him and told him to make urine where he was. My long cardigan was splashed with urine. Another thing for the wash!

I helped him get his knees on the rug and heave himself up with his elbows on the bed. He was really tired. I noticed that his right ankle was very swollen. He has to see the kidney specialist next week. Must remember to get his blood test done.

Friday

Jack took the dogs for a walk round the garden. Madam Almond followed them. Using both elbow crutches, he walked right up, past the pool to the granny cottage, quite a way for him. The dogs came running back to the house, they were so excited. Obviously something was wrong. Megan did her usual tugging at my shoe. I followed them up and found Jack lying on the floor of the cottage. He had fallen against one of the wooden units and cut the side of his face. I managed to get him up on to the wooden unit and he sat there for a while. I rushed back to the house to get the first aid kit, then washed the wound, which wasn't too bad; it certainly wouldn't need stitching. I stuck on a plaster to keep it clean. We walked slowly back to the house. He used an elbow crutch and held on to my arm.

I called the doctor. He advised that we come down to the Salud and have him checked over.

The staff were waiting for us when we arrived. He was X-rayed on his head and there was no damage. The cut was re-examined and it was cleaned and dressed again. The doctor advised me to think about getting a wheel chair because of all the falls.

Jack went straight to bed and slept till dinnertime then ate a hearty meal and was quite back to normal by the time Esther arrived to get him ready for bed.

Saturday

Went down to Muro to do the weekly shop and meet our friends Sue and Paul for lunch. We Ate a beautiful meal at el Restaurante

Cabaza. We sat in the sun and chatted for another hour then returned home for a two hour siesta. Life is so laid back here.

Sunday

Jack is really unwell today. I think he has another urine infection. These have been happening on a regular basis. I called the doctor and he came up to the house. After examination he advised that Jack have further tests. He telephoned for an ambulance.

Jack was taken to the hospital in Alcoy. The diagnosis was a kidney infection and he must be admitted.

He was transferred to the Unidad de Riñón, Kidney Unit. He was very ill and I stayed with him. I telephoned Matthew, our Au Per from Shetland and told him to make some food for himself and please feed the dogs and cats, I may be a while and he would just see me when I arrived.

Thirty one

———— ✦ ————

I went to the pool to give Megan her swim. I saw a three inch dragonfly lying on the surface. It looked dead but I felt impelled to scoop it out in the pool net. It was the first time I have ever held a dragon fly. It was so beautiful. Its four wings felt like exquisitely strong filigree, like they were made of silver wires laid out on glass. The body was a glorious luminescent turquoise blue. I took it into my office and laid it on a folder. I took several photographs.

I had my siesta for about two hours. I went back into my office, I picked up the dragonfly and it curled its little body into a c shape. It was alive!! I held it on the palm of my hand and it slightly fluttered its wings. I felt so elated, happy and grateful for the survival of this wonderful little creature. I sat with it, asking God to please help this little one and it gently moved its body again. I took it outside to the sun to let it warm up. After a minute it fluttered its wings and tried to fly. It was still very weak, so I placed it on the hedge in the warmth. I knew that if it did manage to fly from there, it would have a twenty feet drop to take off from. In a few minutes it took to the air. Swooped down almost to the ground then rose up and eventually disappeared in the olive grove.

I think that this was a sign that however low we get, we can survive and take to the air again. I can still feel the warm tears running down my cheeks as I watched it fly away.

God be with you little one.

Thirty two

———— ◆ ————

Tiggy, a little grey tabby, was Jack's favourite. She had been standoffish from the beginning and it was only by Jack's perseverance and patience (which he had in abundance with the animals) that she eventually became a loving little pussy cat.

Jack would stand for ages holding some cat food between his fingers and saying Tiggy, Tiggy Tiggy, come pussycat. Usually one of the other cats would jump in first and devour it. Eventually Tiggy got the message and Jack became her favourite human. It was a long time later that she allowed Jack to pick her up. She never entered the house and preferred to sleep in a cardboard box beside one of the armchairs on the terrace.

When the time came for us to leave Spain, only two cats remained and we could not bear to leave them behind. They would both come to Scotland. The decision was made to have Tiggy micro chipped, and passported as well as Madam Almond. After attempting with great difficulty to get her into one of the cat cages, Jack suffered numerous scratches on his hands. I was so concerned that he would have problems with the cuts because of his diabetes. I grabbed Tiggy and wrapped her in a thick towel and forced her into the cage. She was absolutely furious. Screaming like a banshee and clawing the edges of the cage, then rolling over and over, trying to tear the towel.

We drove down to Muro; Almu was on Holiday so we took her to Jorge the local vet.

The whole of Muro must have heard her bemoaning the fact that she had a cruel Mummy and Daddy who had shut her up in a cage and dragged her away from her beloved home.

She was a little monster in the surgery. Jorge wrapped her up in the towel to prevent getting torn to shreds and managed to get a muzzle on her.

She was terrified of the electric shaver and went mad, legs everywhere, claws slashing around. She had her micro chip implanted. Poor little Tiggy. When it was all over, she rushed back into the cat mobile, forcing herself against the back of the cage screaming and spitting with her back up. I dreaded to think what she would be like on the journey back to Scotland.

We would have to take her back for her rabies vaccination and then again for the test results before she could travel.

There was no comparison between Tiggy and Madam Almond. Almond was quiet and sedate when in her cage and extremely well behaved with the vets. She would purr through the whole appointment and not a sound came from her when she was in the car.

I had several bad scratches on my hands and a deep bite on the knuckle of my right hand, middle finger. It was painful and woke me up a few times during the night.

I was having my breakfast when I noticed that the veins going up my arm were red. I called the surgery and was told to come straight down. The doctor said I was lucky I had noticed it so soon because Tiggy's bite had become infected. My whole hand and arm were swollen.

I had anti tetanus and antibiotic injections and had to take two antibiotic tablets for eight days. If there was no improvement by the next day, I was to go straight to emergency.

Fortunately the antibiotics were working and the arm felt a lot better two days later.

Jack also had an anti-tetanus injection and had no further problems.

Several days later I was cleaning the pool. Tiggy was sitting on the wall watching me carefully. As I neared the pool end by the big pine trees, she sauntered along the top towards me. I put out my hand to stroke her and she pressed her head hard onto my shoulder, rubbing and purring. This was so unlike Tiggy. She was not usually the cuddly type of puss. I picked her up in my arms and she continued to cuddle into me. I stroked her gently and spoke lovingly to her. She continued to let me spoil her for a few minutes then jumped on to the wall and dropped over the other side.

I told Jack about it and he said Tiggy had come over to him on the terrace and stroked her head against his chest for a few minutes, then wandered over to the old olive tree at the side of the house. He also was surprised because she had never done that to him before.

That was the last time we saw Tiggy. Jack was absolutely distraught. His beautiful stripy Tiggy just disappeared. We never saw her again.

We looked everywhere, calling her name, even made a recording and left it playing on repeat in the garden all night in the hope that she would return, but she never did. Our dear little Tiggy had come to say goodbye and then just disappeared. Now we only had one cat to take back to Scotland.

Thirty three

———— ✦ ————

It was early May; I woke the dogs up to take them outside for their night walk. I stood on the terrace and to my amazement, six little fox cubs ran across the driveway and disappeared into the car port.

The dogs took off at a rate of knots after them. I raced across the drive and plunged into the car port to find the dogs squealing with delight and the fox cubs all huddled together in the corner in front of the car. I pulled the dogs, yelling at them to "leave! Leave! Back off" and dragged them back into the house. They were not amused at being shut away from the excitement and were all barking like mad.

I rushed back to the car port and they were still all there, shaking in terror.

I didn't touch them for fear the mother would reject them if they had my scent. "You just stay there until your Mummy comes to get you" and I walked calmly back to the house. I took the dogs out again but this time they had their leads on and we left by the back door.

In the morning Zanussi bolted out of the door and raced up to the granny flat. I heard a squeal. He came rushing back with a fox cub, carrying it like he would a puppy. He held it gently round the neck. He didn't harm it and dropped it in his big cage on the terrace. "It's mine, it's mine!!" The little creature lay quite still, I thought it was dead. Then I could see it breathing lightly. It was faking! Zanussi kept prodding it's tummy with his nose but it wouldn't get up. I pulled him, with great effort, out of the crate and closed the door. The little cub then lifted his head and looked at me. He got up and started scratching on the side of the crate, squealing and yapping. I shut Zanussi and Megan (who only showed a slight interest) in the house, put on my thick gardening gloves and picked up the cub. It sank its little needle sharp teeth into my hand through the glove, and proceeded to punch away at me for another four bites. Within seconds my glove was red. I put the cub into the cat travel box then took a video of the little creature. I crossed the drive and took the box over to the middle of the groves and opened the door. It stayed motionless. I said, "Now you just wait there until your Mummy comes for you" and I walked away, hoping that Mummy would appear soon.

I came back to the house and phoned the health centre for advice about my puncture bites. The receptionist said "come down to the Salud (health centre) immediately. I got Jack out of bed, rushed him outside and pushed him into the car, still in his pyjamas, he was protesting vigorously while I headed for the Health Centre at top speed. I couldn't see out of the back window for gravel and dust. The outcome was I had to get anti-rabies injections in my butt (and boy did they sting) for five days, lasting to the end of the week and have another one a month later. When I came back home, the cat box on the groves was empty and the little cub was gone. I hoped his Mummy had come for him and he would survive.

Hay Ho!! Just another episode in the quiet life at El Pinar.

I sent an e-mail to my son Michael about the cub and this was his reply.

"That's that bloody Zanussi dog again. How much has he cost you so far?"

Thirty four

———— ◆ ————

T his Christmas we would be on our own. All of our family had visited earlier in the year, so Jack said I was not to spend the time cooking, we would go out for Christmas dinner.

The hotel in the village was only five minutes away in the village. It had a good reputation and advertised that they catered for all diets.

I made the reservation at the beginning of December. I explained to the receptionist that I was a vegetarian but my husband ate meat.

She sent for the chef and he invited us to have coffee while we discussed the menu.

He said he was quite used to cooking vegetarian food and disappeared into the kitchen for a few minutes. He came back with a book of Spanish vegetarian menus.

I checked out some of the menus and told him what I would like. It was a pleasant discussion and he was really interested in hearing about Scotland.

On Christmas day, we arrived half an hour early and were greeted by the staff and the chef who asked me what he could prepare for me. I told him I was surprised that he had not already prepared my food. Did he not

124

remember that we had discussed this on first of December over coffee?

He gave a little laugh and said, "yes," he had forgotten. I said in that case, I hoped he would use his recipe book we had looked at to produce something special for me.

We waited three quarters of an hour and Jack and I sat patiently while the chef prepared my special meal.

Eventually, a raw salad was placed on the table for both of us as a starter.

This was lettuce, sliced tomato and cucumber.

Jack's first course was perfect for him and he ate every bit.

My course was the same vegetables as the salad but chopped finely and pressed into a mould and then upturned on to the centre of a large dinner plate. Not even a garnish.

My second course was plain aubergine, sliced and fried along with a few cold chips and again, no garnish was given. A tasteless, colourless meal. I do not like aubergine.

The dessert for both of us was a slice of fried bread dipped in sugar with a ball of ice cream on the top. The waitress apologized and said that the chef had not had a good day.

I wholeheartedly agreed with her and said we also had not had a good day and asked to see the manager.

He was most apologetic and offered us coffee and ginger cake free of charge. I replied that the gesture would have been acceptable if he had offered the whole meal for free.

On returning home, I was so disappointed I wrote a letter to the hotel manager.

Dear Sir,

I am writing to you to express my gross disapproval of the food which I received, most of which I could not eat. It was a disgusting meal for any day, let alone Christmas. I have never in all my 72 years of life had such a bad, inadequate, Christmas dinner and still had to pay the full price for a few unprepared vegetables and a slice of fried bread with a dab of ice cream. No effort was put into the preparation. I did assume that your chef, as a professional caterer, would be capable of preparing meals for all special diets. A hotel of your caliber should have no problem satisfying all of its customers.

I was the only vegetarian there and felt like an outcast. We sat for 2 and a half hours and for most of the time, I had inedible food. I would also add that the food which my husband received was to a high standard with several more courses than I had received. He was very satisfied with his Christmas lunch.

This was my Christmas menu at your hotel.

Drinks	Aerated water

First course	Cold chopped salad vegetables

Second course   Cold chips and fried sliced aubergine

Dessert   Slice of fried bread with small ball of ice cream.

Total cost ………….. 35 Euros

Do you think that was fair value?

I trust you will reply to my letter and give some explanation for a very poor service. If your hotel is unable to cater for vegetarians, then you should not advertise the fact that you cater for all diets.

May I take this opportunity to wish you and your staff, a very happy New Year and hope that by Christmas 2012, your chef will have had some time to look at a few vegetarian recipe books?

Yours **VERY** sincerely

Edna Clyne Rekhy

I drove down to the hotel again and handed my letter into reception.

About one hour later, I heard the gate bell.

The manager was standing at the gate with a huge bouquet of flowers and several boxes of chocolates and biscuits. He had a huge grin on his face. He said he was so sorry that our Christmas had been ruined and he would like to make things better.

Would we come to the hotel tomorrow evening and he would present us with some better food? He would send a taxi so we could both have a bottle of wine. Of course, I accepted his invitation.

Next evening the taxi arrived at the allotted time and we were chauffeured to the hotel. We were greeted at the door by the manager and the kitchen staff, who all shook our hands and wished us Feliz Navidad (Merry Christmas) We were escorted to our table which was beautifully set with a hand embroidered table cloth, gorgeous china and silver cutlery. Candles were lit and wine brought.

This was my menu.

Starter   Melon, fruit filled boat complete with cheese sails.

Second   Nut loaf with gorgeous tomato salsa and mixed six

                  vegetable salad

Third   Curried chick peas with roast potatoes and mixed roast

Vegetables. (Jack also had this)

Fourth   Grilled stuffed mushrooms with
cream sauce and roast

tomatoes.

Dessert   Coffee cheesecake topped with
fresh cream and

Strawberries.

To finish   Coffee, ginger snaps and Liqueurs

This was most certainly the best vegetarian meal I had ever eaten in any restaurant. It was completely delicious and mouth watering. The presentation was exquisite. Jack's food was also of the highest quality, meeting course for course. We both thanked the manager, the chef and the staff for a wonderful evening and the excellent food

Our taxi was waiting at the door and as we were leaving the Manager said, "I have to tell you, yesterday the chef was suffering from a hangover"

Thirty five

---◆---

My Scottish Holiday.

Things had been a bit difficult and I felt I needed a clean break. Michael and Joanne had invited me over to Scotland for a holiday and I decided to take advantage of this.

I engaged an au pair from Shetland, recommended by Joanne. I had a week to prepare Dianne for being on her own with Jack and the animals. She proved to be an absolute Godsend. She was so patient with Jack and a really lovely person. Always happy and she just adored the animals. I had no reservations about leaving her in charge while I had some respite in Scotland.

My first visit was to Shetland to see Michael and Joanne and enjoy time with my grandchildren, Alex and Erin. They were so pleased to see me "in the flesh at last" as Erin put it. They had come out to Spain on several occasions and thoroughly enjoyed the wonderful weather. Michael especially needed the rest. He is a workaholic and a perfectionist; he probably takes this trait from me. He produces wonderful photography and videos.

The pool was always inviting and we had to take care that the children were watched all the time. I had a builder erect a wall and a strong gate just to be on the safe side but little Erin is a born climber and this gate was a challenge.

Shetland is a so beautiful, it is difficult not to take pictures there. We spent a long time puffin watching on the cliffs at Sumburgh Head and I Managed to take some wonderful photographs. The weather was perfect I didn't miss the Spanish heat.

I then flew to Inverness to my other son Steven and his wife Pat. My grandsons Darren and Kieran were in Spain with their other grandfather and I was really sorry to have missed them. Their holiday had been planned before I decided to come to Scotland. It was wonderful to catch up on all the local news and meet friends I hadn't seen for years.

I took a trip back to Brora, where we had lived for over twenty years and I had my designer tweeds and knitwear business. So nice meet again with all our old neighbours and friends. I was feeling relaxed and rested.

It was time to return to Spain. I flew to Manchester in the morning to catch my connecting flight to Alicante.

Then the phone call came from Michael telling me that Jack was in hospital.

Dianne had called him in Shetland to tell him the news.

I was so worried I didn't sleep a wink. I didn't have a number for the hospital and couldn't contact anyone to find out what was wrong. My mobile phone by this time was out of money. Then I had an alarm call at 4am to get up for my flight leaving at 6.45am.

I couldn't find out what had happened to Jack and made up my mind that he had passed away during the night.

Our friends Jane and Stuart met me at Alicante airport with the news that Jack was okay.

He had been very good for five days, and then all hell broke loose. He fired Katia, our Russian cleaner, told Esther, the nurse, to get out of his house and not come back, shouted at Dianne to clear off back to Scotland and then had to be taken off to hospital by emergency ambulance because he was seeing beetles crawling up everyone's faces.

The hospital doctor thought Jack had possibly taken some medicine he was not supposed to. Anyway, he kicked up such a fuss, disturbing all the other patients that they sent him home at three in the morning.

Dianne in the meantime had stuffed a pair of ear plugs in, trying to get some much needed sleep.

When the ambulance arrived at the house, the paramedics got no reply to either the gate bell or the telephone and they called the police, who, when they arrived, scaled the gate, nearly bashed the bedroom window in trying to waken Dianne and when they eventually got her up, demanded to see her passport and threatened to arrest her for wasting the time of the ambulance men. The poor girl was terrified, eventually they left because Jack ordered them all out of his house, Dianne said he was at least a foot taller than the police and the paramedics and they looked terrified of him.

She was really freaked out by all the fuss and decided to phone Michael in Shetland, who telephoned me in the hotel at Manchester, waiting for my flight in the morning to Alicante. My mobile phone just wouldn't make contact with Spain, so I didn't know if he was alive or dead until I arrived home.

Of course, everything was back to normal the minute I arrived.

Jack told Jane, she could leave now and shut the gate behind her. Stuart told Jack that if he ever spoke to Jane in that manner again, he would give him a wallop. Our friends had been so helpful. They had just taken me home from the airport eighty kilometers away and here he was being abusive towards them. Jane burst into tears and told Stuart off for being bad tempered and they left for home not speaking to each other ever again.

I asked Jack what he thought he was playing at, and he didn't remember a thing. He gave me a big hug and said he was glad I was back home because he hadn't had a decent meal since I left. Diane is a good cook and I knew he had been well fed all the time. Jack had completely forgotten about the ambulance and police and that I had been on holiday and announced that he was going to have a lie down because he was exhausted. He strolled along the terrace with the dogs in pursuit. "Come my babies, time to rest!!" And everybody wonders how I manage to keep my temper!

Such a saga!! Jack has a way of causing absolute panic and leaving everyone concerned in a state of nervous tension and complete stress while he strolls off completely unfazed.

Our friends Isa and Brian took Dianne to the airport in Alicante next morning for her return trip to Shetland and a peaceful life once again on that beautiful Scottish island. I didn't think she would want to come back to Spain again.

I thoroughly enjoyed my short trip to my family and resolved to do my best to get away for a well deserved break at every opportunity.

Things settled back into our everyday normal, or as normal as things can be in our home. I called the insurance company about the back door lock which had been broken when the wind crashed it shut when the police came and the joiner appeared within half an hour and replaced the lock. Yet another problem settled. Jack slept like a baby that night, as did the dogs. I was absolutely bushed and knew nothing until Esther

arrived in the morning to get Jack ready for day care.

Thirty Six

—— ❖ ——

I loved my life in Spain but I was getting increasingly worried about Jack's situation. He was like a two or three year old child. I was his Mummy and he constantly needed my attention.

If I was in another room he would shout my name non- stop getting louder and louder until I had no option but to go to him. If I took the dogs for their walk on the groves he would come outside onto the terrace and shout so loudly, the neighbours would come up to see what was wrong. I didn't take him with me, it was difficult for him to walk on the groves because the ground was uneven and there was a danger of him falling.

It was time to make a really serious decision. I was more and more thinking about returning to Scotland so Jack could communicate better. He was finding it difficult to converse with the Spanish day-care staff and patients and would become increasingly frustrated.

Once or twice I had a telephone call asking me to come and take Jack home because he was too troublesome for the staff to handle him.

He refused to participate in any of the activities and flatly refused to eat his meals. There was the danger that he would have a diabetic hypo. I sat with him for two mornings at day-care to encourage him to join in and to take his morning coffee and lunch. He was fine while I was there but reverted to being difficult when I was not there.

He eventually flatly refused to go back to day-care and there was absolutely nothing I could do to persuade him to return.

I engaged a retired English nurse Mary, to spend time with him while I worked elsewhere in the house.

She was really a great help and kept him amused by doing simple handcrafts, reading to him and taking him down to the village to sit at one of the local cafes and have his coffee and tostadas.

I only used the inside kitchen for about two months of the year, the rest of the time I worked in the summer kitchen which was outside at the back of the house beside the swimming pool. I loved working there and Jack would lie on a pool lounger in the small bower where he could see me.

In the evenings we would sometimes eat there. It was a wooden structure covered in grape vines which I had fitted it out with a table and four olive wood stools I had made from one of the very old trees which came down in a Spring gale. Camilo, our Spanish gardener cut four even lengths of the trunk and I made cushion tops for comfort.

Megan and Puffin used to enjoy this time with us because they could swim around in the pool while we were having our meal. Jack also loved this and was not averse to throwing anything he didn't want to eat, over the pool wall where the dogs would race over the water to grab the scraps before they sank beneath the waves. No matter how often I told Jack not to feed them, he continued and I would spend hours cleaning all the bits off the bottom of the pool with the net. I couldn't dare let him near the pool unless I was there, he could have fallen in and he no longer remembered how to swim. I always put one of the life-jackets on him, just in case.

Our lives out here were ideal except for this dreadful Alzheimer's, so it was time for me to make the big decision to sell the house and return to Scotland.

I contacted the housing agent who dealt with us buying the house and it was on the market within four days.

My next book begins with our return journey to Scotland,

I hope you have enjoyed reading(listening to this) one and will feel like buying my next one.

Printed in Great Britain
by Amazon

20900294R00081